D1212875

VIEW FROM THE SEVENTH FLOOR

OTHER BOOKS BY W. W. ROSTOW

The Stages of Economic Growth
The United States in the World Arena
A Proposal:
  Key to an Effective Foreign Policy
  (with Max Millikan)
An American Policy in Asia
The Prospects for Communist China
  (with R. W. Hatch)

VIEW FROM THE SEVENTH FLOOR

W. W. ROSTOW

Harper & Row, Publishers
New York, Evanston, and London

Grateful acknowledgment is made to *Foreign Affairs* for permission to reprint Chapter 12 entitled "The Third Round" © 1964 by the Council on Foreign Relations, Inc., New York.

LIBRARY OF CONGRESS CATALOG CARD NUMBER: 64-15262

G-O

To
the Members of the Policy Planning Council
past, present, and future

CONTENTS

Preface ix

Part I. Our Global Strategy

1. Introduction 3
2. American Strategy on the World Scene 20
3. Power and Diplomacy 34
4. Ideas and Action 45

Part II. The Atlantic Community: Problems of the North

5. The Atlantic Community: An American View 57
6. The Role of Germany in the Evolution of World Politics 69

Part III. North-South Problems

7. Strategy and Economics 83
8. The Challenge of Democracy in Developing Nations 92
9. Guerrilla Warfare in the Underdeveloped Areas 112
10. The Nationalization of Take-off 121
11. How to Make a National Market 132

Part IV. East-West Problems: The Cold War

12. The Third Round 147
13. The Way to Victory 161

Index 169

PREFACE

When I moved over from the White House staff to the Department of State in December 1961, I asked Mr. Rusk if it would not be wise if his counselor and planner be neither seen nor heard. He suggested that all of us should take our turn in explaining the government's foreign policy to the public; and that I should, in particular, concentrate on trying to make clear the relation of the parts to the whole. What are our broad objectives? How are they linked to what is done from day to day in different parts of the world? How are diplomacy and military policy related?

There is some justice in placing this kind of responsibility on the chairman of the Policy Planning Council, even though the Council's daily work is mainly concrete and pragmatic. Each member of the Council concentrates, at any period of time, on one or two tough major problems. Working with his colleagues in the government who bear operational responsibility, his object is to help design a practical course of action that will make the nation's position on the world scene better in the future. A planner is meant not merely to be an inventor but a participant in the practical tasks of innovation. The Council's collective working agenda, however, stretches over the full range of national security problems—from the political aspects of a nuclear age to economic development; and it touches every region of the world. The Policy Planning Council is, thus, one of the relatively few points in a highly specialized and fragmented structure of government where an over-all view should be developed; and this we try to do.

The present volume reflects the effort to execute Mr. Rusk's instruction. The substance of its chapters was mainly presented, in the first instance, as talks to groups in various parts of the United States, in Great Britain, Belgium, Berlin, Mexico, and Venezuela. Chapter 12 in Part IV was, initially, an article in *Foreign Affairs;* and Chapter 9 in Part III is drawn from the only substantial public statement made by me when working in the White House as Deputy Special Assistant to the President for National Security Affairs—a graduation speech to a class made up mainly of foreign military students at Fort Bragg, concentrating on problems of dealing with Communist techniques of subversion and guerrilla warfare.

The structure of the volume follows the terms in which we tend broadly to think of the nation's problems. Part I lays out the broad lines of the nation's strategy and the basic view taken of the relation between force and diplomacy. Part II deals with United States relations with the more advanced nations of the free world and our efforts to build an effective global partnership to supplant the immediate postwar relationship of acute dependence on the United States. These are, broadly speaking, problems of the North. Part III deals with North-South relations; that is, problems of policy toward the governments and peoples of Latin America, Africa, the Middle East, and Asia, whose societies are at an earlier stage in the process of absorbing and applying the fruits of modern science and technology and which are undergoing profound changes that make them peculiarly vulnerable to Communist tactics of penetration, subversion, and insurrection. Part IV comes to rest on the cold war—on East-West relations.

This sequence underlines an important fact: While dealing with the inescapable reality of Communist aggression and other aspects of East-West relations, our main purposes as a nation on the world scene are positive and constructive. Only such a stance promises, in fact, peaceful victory in the cold war.

These views were expressed over a three-year period of rapid change on the world scene. Modern history offers few more dramatic shifts than that from the confident, aggressive, and fast-moving Communist offensive of the early months of 1961 to the still dangerous but fundamentally defensive disarray of the Communist world in the winter of 1963. Throughout this period the objectives, policies, and broad lines of action of the United States have remained steady; but the Introduction in Part I is designed to offer one perspective, from within the government, on how the sequence of events unfolded.

It goes without saying that this book owes a great deal to the work and insights of my colleagues on the Policy Planning Council, and, indeed, to many other colleagues—military and civilian—with whom I have the privilege of working. But following the tradition of individual responsibility which we seek to cultivate in the planning business, these are my own efforts to articulate the policy on the world scene defined by President Kennedy, reaffirmed and carried forward by President Johnson, and executed within the Department of State by Secretary of State Rusk.

I owe a special debt to Ernest K. Lindley who, in the midst of most pressing duties as both a Special Assistant to the Secretary of State and a member of the Policy Planning Council, found the time to edit and to give order to these papers.

W. W. Rostow

Washington, D. C.
February 1964

Part I

Our Global Strategy

I Introduction

The chapters that follow elaborate two grand themes which arose from the times with which they are concerned and the manner in which they were met by the nation's leaders.

The first is the short-run problem—the turning back of the great post-Sputnik Communist offensive whose contours took shape between 1953 and 1958, which radically accelerated after the launching of the first satellite in October 1957, which was still moving forward with evident momentum in January 1961, and which was brought to a virtual halt between, roughly, May 1961 and October 1962.

President Kennedy, in the Foreword to his *Public Papers* for 1962 wrote:

> Future historians, looking back at 1962, may well mark this year as the time when the tide of international politics began at last to flow strongly toward the world of diversity and freedom. Following the launching of Sputnik in 1957, the Soviet Union began to intensify its pressures against the non-communist world—especially in Southeast Asia, in Central Africa, in Latin America and around Berlin. The notable Soviet successes in space were taken as evidence that communism held the key to the scientific and technological future. People in many countries began to accept the notion that communism was mankind's inevitable destiny.
>
> 1962 stopped this process.

The Cuba missile crisis of October was, evidently, an historical benchmark in this great turn-around. But as early as March 23, 1962, speaking at Berkeley, California—fourteen months after his inaugural—President Kennedy reflected a sense that the tide was already turning.

> There used to be so much talk a few years ago about the inevitable triumph of communism. We hear such talk much less now. No one who examines the modern world can doubt that the great currents of history are carrying the world away from the monolithic idea towards the pluralistic idea—away from communism and towards national independence and freedom. No one can doubt that the wave of the future is not the conquest of the world by a single dogmatic creed but the liberation of the diverse energies of free nations and free men.

And then he went on to the second theme:

> Beyond the drumfire of daily crisis, therefore, there is arising the outlines of a robust and vital world community, founded on nations secure in their own independence, and united by allegiance to world peace. It would be foolish to say that this world will be won tomorrow, or the day after. The processes of history are fitful and uncertain and aggravating. There will be frustrations and setbacks. There will be times of anxiety and gloom. The specter of thermonuclear war will continue to hang over mankind. . . .
>
> Yet we can have a new confidence today in the direction in which history is moving. . . .
>
> . . . We must seize the vision of a free and diverse world—and shape our policies to speed progress toward a more flexible world order.
>
> This is the unifying spirit of our policies in the world today.

The second theme of this book embraces specific dimensions of the building of "a robust and vital world community": the problems of partnership with Europe and Japan; of building a new and constructive relation between the developing nations and the more advanced nations of the free world; of moving, as opportunity may offer, to agreements with Communist states which yield a margin of increased security for all; and of underpinning the whole difficult and hazardous historical process with the scale and types of military force which would not merely protect us but which promise as stable a military environment as is possible.

II

This counterpoint between a tense and desperate short-run struggle and the longer rhythm of construction on many fronts constitutes, evidently, one of the great enterprises in the nation's history; but it is an enterprise different from those which we have in the past designated as "great."

In this century we generally think of "great" periods under two sets of circumstances.

The first were intervals in domestic policy when there occurred a sudden outpouring of major new legislation, with permanent consequences for the organization of our society. Since 1900 there were two such intervals: the legislative execution of Wilson's concept of the "New Freedom" during his first term; and the vast flow of New Deal legislation in Franklin Roosevelt's first term.

Theodore Roosevelt's administrations should, I believe, be added to the list of great periods, although new legislation actually passed in his time was limited. He nevertheless, laid the groundwork for new attitudes and policies, at home and abroad, which foreshadowed many fundamental later developments.

The second phases of greatness in the twentieth century were occasions of desperate crisis on the international scene. Theodore Roosevelt's effort to educate the nation to the vistas of world power and responsibility had not sufficiently succeeded. In 1917 the United States had to go to war to avoid the passage of power in western Europe and in the Atlantic to forces hostile to the United States and its way of life. Thus we undid our previous commitment to isolationism. In 1941, with the passage of lend lease and, then, our full engagement after Pearl Harbor, we again had to salvage vital American interests by engaging in a world conflict, once again undoing a prior national commitment to isolationism. In 1947 we had to reverse the course of immediate postwar policy in order to salvage and protect Western Europe and the balance of world power. In June 1950 we had to go to war in Korea to meet a major act of Communist aggression and repair the weakness of our conventional military establishment in the Far East, which, in turn, resulted from our relatively low postwar military budgets.

The great periods in executive leadership in this century have, thus, been periods where radical action was taken at home to correct previous distortions in our policy or to cope with desperate crises abroad.

III

The Kennedy administration came to responsibility at a time when major new initiatives were, indeed, required both at home and abroad; but in neither domestic nor foreign affairs had these problems reached a stage of overwhelming crisis. Without the stimulus of major crises and the consensus that major crises bring about in our sturdy national community, the task of American leadership has been, both at home and abroad, to bring about movement toward large objectives by small increments over considerable periods of time.

In domestic affairs it has taken sustained executive leadership, as well as protracted advocacy and debate, to move policy in the directions Presidents Kennedy and Johnson have sought to move with respect to race relations, wages, prices, business expansion, education, and medical care for the aged.

Abroad, President Kennedy faced in January 1961 a series of dangerous and degenerative crises and the need, as well, to shift the direction of policy with respect to Western Europe and Japan; with respect to Latin America; with respect to the underdeveloped areas of Africa, the Middle East, Asia; with respect to our military capacity; and, if possible, with respect to the problem of bringing the arms race under control. It was his objective to bring about an improvement in the free world's position in the cold war, if possible without war. And it was of the nature of the constructive problems within the free world that slow, irregular movement forward, in small steps, over substantial periods of time, was what the situation permitted and required.

IV

But first—and urgently—there was the problem of the cold war itself. In 1957, four years after Stalin's death, Khrushchev had finally consolidated his control over both the Communist party and the Soviet government. He was the unquestioned master of affairs in Moscow. With the launching of the first Sputnik in October 1957, he also launched at full tilt the second great Communist offensive of the postwar years—the first being Stalin's, which was frustrated in the West with the success of the Berlin airlift in 1949 and in the East with the defeat of the Chinese Communist armies at the thirty-eighth parallel in April–May 1951.

Khrushchev sought to use the image of Soviet nuclear strength and its capacity to destroy Western Europe with medium range ballistic missiles to blackmail the West into surrendering West Berlin.

In the underdeveloped areas of Asia, the Middle East, Africa, and Latin America, Moscow sought to extend its power by orchestrating the instruments of guerrilla warfare, subversion, trade, and aid; by appealing to anticolonial and nationalist sentiments; and by projecting an image of communism as the most efficient method for modernizing the underdeveloped region and as a system closing rapidly on the sluggish American front runner.

In January 1961 the 1958 Berlin ultimatum was still on the books, and increasing pressure was being applied against the West. The situation in Southeast Asia was rapidly deteriorating, from Vientiane to Djakarta. The Communist threat to the Congo was not under control; and Castro was casting a dangerous spell on all Latin America. The cause of freedom appeared widely to be on the defensive.

The shift in the balance of the cold war since January 1961 is quite as dramatic as any we have seen in modern times. But this shift was not brought about by a war or by any single incident or crisis. It was brought about by a series of military and political moves, each difficult and protracted, each involving moments of hazard, climaxed, of course, by the Cuba missile crisis of October 1962. This slow-moving turn in the tide must, therefore, be marked off by a series of events, not a single great turning point.

Acknowledging the limitations of historical perspective with which such recent events must be judged, here is a tentative list of crucial turning points:

Laos, May 1961. A ceasefire was finally implemented after President Kennedy ordered the loading of the Marines in the Pacific to prepare to take up positions in Laos and indicated to Moscow that he was unwilling to accept a conference on Southeast Asia at Geneva while the war in Laos continued. (In 1954 the French defeat at Dien Bien Phu occurred during the Geneva Conference.)

Berlin, July 1961. After his Vienna conference with Khrushchev, with its virtual Berlin ultimatum, President Kennedy committed the United States to use all forces at our command to defend Western vital interests in Berlin, asking (and receiving from the Congress) a further rise in the military budget which brought the 1961 increase to $6 billion.

Vietnam, December 1961. President Kennedy ordered a radical increase in our military and civil support for South Vietnam after General Maxwell Taylor's report in November 1961; a period of dangerous deterioration in the situation was ended; and the basis was laid for some eighteen months of progress.

Cuba, January 1962. The Punta del Este conference of the Organization of American States declared that the present government of Cuba was incompatible with the hemispheric organization; ejected that government from the OAS; and adopted resolutions for collective defense against Communist penetration of the hemisphere, which served as the base for hemispheric solidarity in the missile crisis later in the year.

Berlin, February–March 1962. The Communist attempt to crack the unity of the Western alliance by intruding into the air corridors to Berlin was frustrated by cool and united Allied behavior rooted in contingency plans agreed on in advance.

West New Guinea, August 1962. The Netherlands and Indonesia successfully negotiated a settlement of the West New Guinea question with the assistance of Ambassador Ellsworth Bunker, opening the way to improved relations between Indonesia and the West and frustrating Moscow's plans.

Cuba, October 1962. Soviet offensive missiles were discovered being emplaced in Cuba; a selective blockade was established with OAS and NATO support; the missiles were withdrawn by Khrushchev.

The Congo, January 1963. Capture of Jadotville by United Nations forces led to agreement on Congolese unity and to reconciliation between Belgium and the Central government of the Congo.

It was our assessment in the Policy Planning Council, as of late August 1962, that the men in Moscow would have judged that the post-Sputnik offensive was failing. It was further assessed that Moscow was unlikely to accept this failure passively; and we worked during September on the assumption that we were about to see perhaps the greatest act of risk-taking since the war, in an attempt to retrieve a waning Communist position. We estimated that there were three points of danger: Berlin; Cuba; and an effort by Moscow to produce what would be—or would appear to be—a favorable shift in the nuclear balance.

We considered the installation of offensive missiles in Cuba, although we did not predict it because we judged it would be a most unwise and risky act—which, indeed, it was.

Nevertheless, the attempt to install the offensive missiles in Cuba combined all three objectives we had contemplated. If we had accepted those missiles, their presence in Cuba would have been, from Moscow's point of view, the best possible background for pressure on Berlin; sitting under our early warning net, they would have produced a limited but significant shift in the nuclear balance; and they would have given substance to the image of communism as the wave of the future in Latin America and in other underdeveloped areas. When the American response forced the removal of missiles from Cuba, Moscow's post-Sputnik offensive was over.

Several things need to be said about this sequence. First, no one in the Executive Branch believes that the crises in Cuba, in Southeast Asia, or elsewhere have been ended; and it is open to the Soviet Union, if it accepts new risks, to resume new offensives. There is no tendency in Washington to throw our hats in the air. What has happened is that an extremely dangerous set of intrusions into the free world, which occurred in the three years after the launching of the first Sputnik, and which were not under control in January 1961, have been brought more nearly under control. The Communist thrust initiated in 1958 has lost its momentum. A phase in the cold war has ended. The men in Moscow must, evidently, decide where they go from here; and we must be prepared for a possible resumption of a Communist offensive, on new lines or on the old, as well as for the possibility of moving toward a relaxation of danger and tension.

In this critical interval of choice, President Kennedy spoke the nation's desire for a world at peace in his speech at American University and dispatched Governor Harriman to Moscow. The atmospheric test ban, the hot line agreement, the banning of weapons from outer space, and several lesser moves were accomplished; but Moscow has thus far been unwilling to face and solve the fundamental issues of the cold war. As of early 1964, the terrain of negotiation and the range of agreement remained exceedingly narrow; but President Johnson is evidently alert to specific possibilities for widening that terrain.

The second thing to be said about this sequence is that, while the actions of the United States and its allies have been important in bringing about this slow but dramatic turn, other forces, both outside the Communist bloc and within it, have contributed: notably the determination and skill of the developing nations in defending their independence against Communist intrusions and blandishments; the rise of nationalism within the Communist world; and the emergence of deeply rooted economic difficulties, industrial as well as agricultural, from East Germany to Communist China.

This whole turn-around effort was given substance and support by a radical strengthening of the American military posture: a 50 per cent increase in the Polaris submarine program; a very significant increase in the number of Minuteman missiles; a 50 per cent increase in the number of our strategic bombers on fifteen-minute ground alert; an increase in our combat-ready Army divisions from eleven to sixteen; a very substantial increase in the size of our airlift and sealift; and a new and major effort on behalf of both the civil and military parts of our government to cope with Communist techniques of subversion, insurrection, and guerrilla warfare. But no amount of additional military hardware would have helped us if the Communists were not convinced that we would use American military force to defend vital interests of the free world. They came to that understanding at one point after another; and their assessment was correct.

In addition, Colonel John Glenn's successful orbital flight (February 1962) and the massive increase in the United States space program sharply diluted the political and psychological advantage Moscow had gained by the vigorous exploitation of its big booster over the previous five years.

Whether the shift in the balance of the cold war brought about in the period 1961–1963 will rank with the other great efforts of executive leadership in our history remains to be seen. The problems of Cuba and Southeast Asia are still acute, as President Johnson noted in his State of the Union message of January 1964. The issue raised in Chapter 9, pages 118–119 has not yet been solved by the world community; namely, the illegal crossing of frontiers with men and arms in support of Communist insurrection. Moreover, the success of the West in dealing with the post-Sputnik offensive released narrow nationalist impulses in many parts of the world, yielding a spate of dangerous regional conflicts. And it is still uncertain whether the next phase of Communist policy will move toward aggression at higher degrees of risk than those already undertaken, or whether we shall move toward a long-term easing of cold war tensions. What can be said is that by the patient and protracted application of American military and diplomatic power we substantially reversed a Communist offensive which, between 1958 and 1961, had reached very dangerous proportions indeed.

But even more was involved in turning back Moscow's post-Sputnik offensive. The acquisition by Moscow of a capacity to destroy western Europe and to do vast damage directly to the United States raised a new hope in the Communist world, a new fear in the West: Would the United States—and the West—have the courage to act with military force against limited Communist thrusts, when that response risked escalation to nuclear war? Could we be blackmailed by the shadow of nuclear war into a succession of limited surrenders? This tactic evidently lay behind Moscow's Berlin policy and its effort to thrust missiles into Cuba. This vision evidently lay behind Mao's post-Sputnik cry: "The East Wind is prevailing over the West

Wind." It had to be answered if our alliances were to survive and, indeed, if there was to be any chance of Moscow accepting the limitations of the world as it is and moving toward peace.

As nearly as history affords a clear answer, it was given by the United States and its allies in, roughly, the year and a half leading up to the Cuba missile crisis of October 1962. If we of the free world keep our nerve and will, nuclear blackmail as a technique of diplomacy may well be judged counterproductive in the future.

V

But reversing a Communist offensive is, evidently, not enough. The world of free men must demonstrate not only that it can assure its survival but that it can creatively solve its problems.

Despite the burden and urgency of the multiple crises on the nation's agenda as of January 1961, President Kennedy launched a series of long-run constructive moves on the international scene in response to slow but dangerous erosion within the free world.

We needed, for example, a policy which would align the United States actively with the great forces in Latin America which seek economic development and greater social justice. To this our response was the Alliance for Progress.

We also needed a foreign aid program capable of aligning the United States with similar forces in Asia, the Middle East, and Africa. In those vast regions peoples and governments are determined to develop their status as independent nations and to provide for themselves and their children an environment of economic growth, progress, and human dignity. Our response was a foreign aid program designed to help nations that showed a capacity and effective will to mobilize their own energies and resources for the development of their societies.

Our aid program is rooted in the sound principle of self-help. It is designed to reward those who show a capacity and a will to help themselves. Along with our Atlantic partners and Japan, we hope gradually to build a stable relationship in which we can work together with the new and aspiring nations as each of them goes forward to the stage where it can qualify for this type of long-run development assistance.

The Peace Corps we have developed—and those generated in its wake in other countries—is both the symbol of free world policy designed to harmonize the interests of the more developed and less developed nations, and a significant part of its substance. As (then) Vice President Johnson said, in October 1962, speaking at a conference on the Peace Corps concept in Puerto Rico: "The key to success within a developing nation lies not merely in the realm of technical activity. Beyond that, it lies in bringing the city folk and the country people, the rich and the poor, the scholar and the illiterate into a sense of common purpose and common nationhood."

With respect to Western Europe, we found that the success of the nation's policies over the fifteen years since the war had faced us with two massive facts which we had to take actively into account.

First, Western Europe in the 1950s experienced an extraordinary surge of growth and development and was eager to accept a new degree of authority over its own destiny.

Second, the movement toward European unity—which we had helped foster immediately after the war—had gained real momentum. A united Europe had become a real possibility, but its shape and our policy toward its evolution were not yet determined. With respect to Japan, we found that our policies had not fully taken into account Japan's impulse—after a decade of growth quite as remarkable as that of Western Europe—to find a new role of dignity and responsibility on the world scene.

We are in the midst of the laborious but critically important process of working out the terms of partnership in military matters, in trade, in problems of currency and reserves, in aiding the underdeveloped areas, and in the field of intensified political consultation. Despite the frustration of British entry into the Common Market and the continuing debate on the future structure of the Atlantic Alliance, we have quietly made limited progress on all these fronts.

Similarly, we are working with the government of Japan, with the leaders of Japanese society—at every level—and with our friends in the Atlantic Community to help weave the great potential contribution of Japan into the fabric of the free world's constructive enterprises.

Finally, President Kennedy, conscious of the dangers to the United States and to all inhabitants of the planet that derive from the nuclear arms race and the tendency for an increasing number of countries to enter the nuclear business, created, with Congressional support, the Arms Control and Disarmament Agency. He sought a complete nuclear test ban under dependable conditions of inspection and verification. The atmospheric test ban treaty was achieved. In the meanwhile we have done a great deal to strengthen the capacity of the United Nations to curb aggression, keep the peace, and direct the world community toward the habit of peaceful settlement of international disputes.

It is too soon to judge the outcome of the policies of the Kennedy and Johnson administrations with respect to the Atlantic partnership and Japan, with respect to the Alliance for Progress and our relations with other underdeveloped areas, and with respect to the control of nuclear arms. The objectives set are, clearly, "great" objectives by any standards of the past; but the problems we have set out to solve cannot yield to sudden, dramatic, frontal attack. They require for solution new relations among governments and peoples, and reach deep into the domestic political life of nations where, as we know from our own experience, attitudes change slowly. In a world which has moved beyond its initial postwar stage, when power was concentrated overwhelmingly in Moscow and Washington, we are seeking to organize a community of self-respecting nation-states which would permit its citizens to live in an environment of peace and progress.

As of the winter of 1963–1964 we are conscious, in all these directions, of some movement forward and many still unsolved problems. The Alliance for Progress, for example, has started slowly. As President Kennedy indicated from the beginning, it is to be looked on as a decade's effort at least; and there will be difficulties and mutual adjustments required as in the unfolding of any great partnership venture. On the other hand, beneath the surface, forces within Latin America, working toward economic development and social justice, are gathering strength; the number of serious development programs, new tax programs, new efforts at housing, education, welfare being started, is increasing. Above all, one can see in Latin America, as one assesses the attitudes of the generations, that the younger men and women are increasingly committed to Alliance for Progress goals. Something of the same is true of our efforts at partnership within the West and with Japan and, perhaps, even in our efforts to negotiate control over the nuclear arms race with the Soviet Union. Time and the attitudes of the coming generation are generally with us.

Thus, while final results have not been reached, these have not been paper programs nor policies of exhortation and rhetoric. We have moved some distance down long roads; toward a binding up into partnership of the more advanced nations of the free world, across the Atlantic and the Pacific; toward new relations of dignity and collaboration within the free world between the advanced nations of the North and the developing nations to the South; toward a definite frustration of the Communist thrust; and toward the exploration of the possibilities of controlling the dangers posed for humanity by the existence of nuclear weapons. What is required both within the government and in our country as a whole is the will and the capacitiy to persist.

In the past it has been our national style to let foreign policy problems build up to major crisis proportions and then plunge in to deal with them. In a nuclear age this is a particularly dangerous way to do business. What we need now are new steadiness, patience, and a stubborn sense of direction. In all conscience, the world is complicated and dangerous enough to ensure that crises will, nevertheless, arise. But our objectives will prove attainable if we bring to them the mood of the old schoolyard game of Indian wrestling, where victory went to him who summoned the extra moment of endurance.

VI

Thus, in foreign policy (and much the same could be said of domestic policy) the great objectives of the Kennedy and Johnson administrations have been defined; movement forward has begun; but the objectives have not yet been fully attained.

At home and abroad, to move by a succession of small steps has required clarity about objectives amid much inertia, opposition and confusion. It has required a capacity to accept crises and setbacks arising from the turbulence of a world scene which the United States by no means wholly controls. It has required, above all, stubborn pressure and the steady application of great energy over sustained periods of time to achieve a sequence of limited movements forward, rather than grand breakthroughs in the form of a flood of revolutionary legislation or war.

Three years out, our feeling is that we are in midpassage. Both abroad and at home we have made much more progress than is, perhaps, generally realized; but there is distance to travel before the great objectives defined by Presidents Kennedy and Johnson, to which we remain committed and toward which we have moved, can be set down in the records of history as substantially accomplished.

That is how it looks to one working member of the administration. In our democracy the definitive judgments are rendered by those outside rather than inside the government; and that is, of course, how it should be.

But what I would say with confidence as an historian is this: To assess this kind of sustained effort over a wide front, which we carry forward and wish to carry forward without the stimulus of great domestic crises at home or war abroad, requires somewhat different standards than our historians or political scientists normally apply to the assessment of whether an administration is meeting its duty to history and the American people.

The frontiers of the past were probed, explored, and consolidated by stubborn protracted enterprise, not by the convulsive reaction to crisis; and this is the way it is—and should be—with the new frontiers of the 1960s.

In the early days of the Kennedy administration I remember thinking of the situation as it then looked—especially in foreign affairs—as one in which our job was to deal with an automobile with weak brakes on a hill. It was slowly sliding backward. If we applied enormous energy, we would gradually slow that downward slide and bring the car to a halt. If we continued to apply the same stubborn energy, the car would begin to move forward and, in time, we would get it up to the top of the hill.

Looking back from the vantage point of February 1964, I would say that the backward slide has been halted; forward movement has begun, and can be sustained if we face and surmount the problems posed for us in Southeast Asia and the Caribbean; but the top of the hill has not yet been attained.

Much has been accomplished; but if our large hopes are to be fulfilled and great objectives reached, we must work to a longer rhythm than has been usual in our history.

If we in the United States do a job that lies wholly within our capacity and if the free world maintains a reasonable degree of unity and common purpose, the events, decisions, and initiatives launched in the period 1961–1963 could mark the beginning of the end of the cold war.

The Cuba missile crisis of 1962 could emerge as the Gettysburg of that global civil conflict. We owe it to all free men —and to the memory of President Kennedy—to labor to make it so.

II *American Strategy on the World Scene*

The predominating news which comes to us from day to day—in the newspapers, over television and radio—is the news of crises: Berlin and the Congo; Laos and Vietnam; and all the others. These crises are very much part of the reality we face. But our strategy goes beyond the crises that are forced upon us. We have a clear and constructive strategy. This strategy goes forward in quiet ways which do not make exciting news. Nor is this forward movement always easy to measure.

My main purpose here is to try to explain what it is that we are trying to achieve on the world scene as a nation—positively and constructively—and what our prospects appear to be.

When the Kennedy administration came to responsibility it confronted situations of acute crisis in Southeast Asia, in the Congo, in Cuba, as well as the threat which has overhung Berlin since 1958—Mr. Khrushchev's threat that he would make a separate German treaty which, in his view, would extinguish Western rights in West Berlin. These were by no means the first crises of the postwar years. Such crises have been the lot of all who have borne responsibility in Washington since 1945.

Why is it that we appear to be living in a sea of troubles? What is it that determines the chronic recurrence of crises in our environment?

Leaving aside the direct instrusions of Communist military power in the postwar years—symbolized, for example, by the blockade of Berlin in 1948–1949, the invasion of South Korea in 1950, and the periodic attacks on the offshore islands—postwar crises have been of three kinds, usually in some sort of combination: international crises arising from internal struggles for power, reflecting the inevitable political and social strains of modernization going forward in the underdeveloped areas; colonial or postcolonial conflicts involving European nations on the one hand and the nations and territories of the southern continents on the other; and the Communist efforts systematically to exploit the opportunities offered by these two inherent types of trouble. Think back and you will, I think, agree: Indochina, Suez, Iraq, Cuba, Algeria, the Congo, Bizerte, Goa, West New Guinea, the Dominican Republic. They were all compounded of some combination of these three elements, and they all arose in what we call the underdeveloped areas.

In Stalin's time the main thrust of Communist policy was fairly direct and military; but in the last decade the Communists have worked systematically to make the most of the inevitable turbulence of the modernization process on the one hand and of the North-South conflicts on the other—using that shorthand geographical designation to represent the approximate fact that the industrial revolution came first to the northern portions of the world and is only now gathering strength to the south.

For example, in order to maximize the chance that Indonesia would go to war in order to acquire the Dutch-held territory of West New Guinea, the Communists advanced credits of about a billion dollars to Djakarta, just as, starting in 1955, they granted substantial arms credits in the Middle East to disrupt this area and to align themselves and the local Communist parties with issues that had strong national appeal.

Communist activity is global and is not, of course, confined to arms deals. There is almost literally no nation in Asia, the Middle East, Africa, and Latin America in which the Communists are not investing significant resources in order to organize individuals and groups for the purpose of overthrowing the existing governments and supplanting them with Communist regimes; and they look quite openly to what they call wars of national liberation—that is, to systematic subversion building up to urban insurrection or guerrilla warfare—as a way of bringing communism to the underdeveloped areas. Khrushchev has stated that he regards it as legitimate for Communist regimes to support such insurrection, which we can see in full cry in South Vietnam—a guerrilla war instigated, supplied, and guided from outside the country. In a speech of December 2, 1961, Castro spoke of guerrilla warfare as the match to be thrown into the haystack, and noted that many Latin American countries were ready for such treatment.

It is not difficult to see why the Communists look on the underdeveloped areas as an arena of opportunity. The process of modernization involves radical change not merely in the economy of underdeveloped nations but in their social structure and political life. We live, quite literally, in a revolutionary time. We must expect over the next decade recurrent turbulence in these areas; we must expect systematic efforts by the Communists to exploit this turbulence; we must expect from time to time that crises will occur; and a great deal of skill, courage, and insight will be required to handle them in ways which do not damage—and if possible promote—the interests of the free world.

But our strategy is not built on a merely defensive reaction to these turbulent situations and the Communist effort to exploit them. We are, I think, learning better how to anticipate crises; and we are working with our friends in the free world to head off or to deal with Communist efforts to exploit them. But we are doing more than that, and we intend to do more. We are working to a positive strategy which takes into account the forces at work in our environment and seeks to shape them constructively to our own purposes and interests—as a nation and as members of a community committed to the principles of national independence and human freedom.

What are these fundamental forces which we confront and which we must shape?

—The revolution in military technology, yielding an uncontrolled competitive arms race and, at present, an imbalance of the offensive over the defensive in the field of nuclear weapons.

—The revolution of modernization in Latin America, Africa, Asia, and the Middle East, including the modernization going forward in underdeveloped areas under Communist control.

—The revival of economic momentum and political strength in Western Europe and Japan.

—The revolution in science and technology, notably in international communications.

—The political revolution, marked simultaneously by proliferation of ardent new nations and an intensified interdependence which requires the individual nation-state to cooperate increasingly with others in order to provide for its security and economic welfare.

Taken together, these forces decree a world setting where power and influence are being progressively diffused within, as well as without, the Communist bloc; where strong inhibitions exist against all-out use of military force; where the interaction of societies and sovereign nations becomes progressively more intimate.

In the light of this view of what we confront in the world around us, our strategy has five dimensions.

First, we are strengthening the bonds of association among the more industrialized nations which lie mainly in the northern portion of the free world: Western Europe, Canada, and Japan.

Western Europe and Japan have been caught up in a remarkable phase of postwar recovery and economic growth. During that period they were protected by American military strength and supported in many ways by American economic resources. Although they must still rely on the deterrent power of American nuclear resources, they are evidently entering a phase where they wish to play a larger role on the world scene and have the resources to do so. We are in the midst of an exciting and complicated process of working out new terms of partnership with Western Europe in every dimension.

The European role in nuclear affairs is expanding in the light of Soviet possession of nuclear weapons and missiles, and Moscow's recurrent threat that Western Europe is "hostage" to its missiles.

New patterns of trade are being worked out within Europe, between Europe and the United States, between the whole Atlantic Community and the rest of the world.

Our policies with respect to economic growth and currency reserves are being discussed and aligned in the Organization for Economic Cooperation and Development; and we are moving into a new partnership in the business of aid to the underdeveloped areas.

Although Japan stands in a somewhat different relation to us than does Europe with respect to military affairs, in each of the other dimensions of alliance policy—trade, reserves, and aid—it is moving into a role of partnership with the industrialized north. And bilaterally we have moved closer to Japan, with the visits to Washington of Prime Minister Ikeda, Attorney General Kennedy's visit to Japan, and the meetings of the Joint Committee of Cabinet Ministers of the two nations.

The constructive steps that mark this process of mobilizing strength and resources of the advanced nations of the free world for global tasks do not usually make headlines unless—as is inevitable—there are phases of disagreement along the way; but it is a rapidly developing piece of history which will give to the cause of freedom a new strength, a new bone structure. The Trade Expansion Act of 1962 is both a symbol of what we are trying to create and a crucial element in its architecture.

The second dimension of our strategy concerns our posture

toward the revolution of modernization going forward in Latin America, Africa, Asia, and the Middle East.

What we sometimes call underdeveloped nations represent a wide spectrum with different problems marking each stage along the road to self-sustained growth. Some of these nations are well along the road; others are just beginning. And in the end, each nation, like each individual, is, in an important sense, unique. What is common throughout these regions is that men and women are determined to bring to bear what modern science and technology can afford in order to elevate the standards of life of their peoples and to provide a firm basis for positions of national dignity and independence on the world scene.

The United States is firmly committed to support this effort. We look forward to the emergence of strong assertive nations which, out of their own traditions and aspirations, create their own forms of modern society. We take it as our duty—and our interest—to help maintain the integrity and the independence of this vast modernization process—insofar as our resources and our ability to influence the course of events permit.

In 1961 the Executive Branch and the Congress collaborated to launch a new program which would grant aid increasingly on the basis of each nation's effort to mobilize its own resources. This approach to the development problem—which looks to the creation of long-term national development programs—is beginning to take hold. We are in the midst of a complex turnaround—affecting both our own policy and that of many other nations.

National development plans cannot be made effective by writing them down in government offices; they require effective administration and the mobilization of millions of men and women.

New roads and dams, schools and factories require feasibility studies and blueprints if they are to be built—not merely listing in hopeful government documents. This turn-around process will, therefore, take time; but from one end of the underdeveloped regions to the other it is actively under way.

More than that, it is now clear that the United States is positively aligned with those men and women who do not merely talk about economic development and the modernization of their societies, but who really mean it and are prepared to dedicate their lives to its achievement.

It is no accident that President Kennedy spoke of a "decade of development." We are up against a longer and tougher job than the Marshall Plan. But we have already begun to create a new basis of partnership not merely between ourselves and the underdeveloped areas, but between the whole industrialized northern part of the free world and its less developed regions.

Our objective is to see emerge a new relation of cooperation among self-respecting sovereign nations to supplant the old colonial ties which are gone or fast disappearing from the world scene. While the headlines have been filled with the residual colonial problems—and they are very real—quiet but real progress has been made in fashioning new links between the more developed and the less developed areas.

The building of this new North-South tie is the third major dimension of our strategy on the world scene. It goes forward in the Alliance for Progress; in our relations with the new African nations; in the meetings of the Development Assistance Committee of the OECD in Paris; in the consortium arrangements of the International Bank for Reconstruction and Development; in the transformed relations of the British Commonwealth and the French Community; in the enlarging contribution of Germany, Japan, and other nations to economic development. And, above all, it goes forward in the minds of citizens in both the North and the South who are gradually coming to perceive that—however painful the memories of the colonial past may be—major and abiding areas of common interest are emerging between nations at different stages of the growth process, nations that are authentically committed to the goals of national independence and human freedom.

The fourth dimension of our strategy is military. There is much for us to build within the free world; but we must protect what we are building, or there will be no freedom.

A persistent characteristic of Communist strategy has been its searching attention to specific gaps—regional and technical—in the defenses of the free world. It has been, thus far, an evident purpose of Communist strategy to avoid a direct confrontation not only with United States main strength, but with positions of relative strength within the free world.

Soviet policy appears to be based on sustained and sophisticated study of particular areas of vulnerability (e.g., northern Azerbaijan, Greece, Berlin, Indochina, South Korea) and particular types of vulnerability (e.g., the geographical position of Berlin, the shortage of local defenses against guerrilla warfare in Laos and South Vietnam).

We cannot rule out that in the future the Communists will be prepared to assault directly the United States or other positions of evident strength within the free community. Therefore, it is a first charge on United States military policy to make such direct assault grossly unattractive and unprofitable. But a major lesson of postwar history is that United States and Allied policy must achieve, to the maximum degree possible, a closing off of areas of vulnerability, if we wish to minimize the number and effectiveness of Communist probes. It is this lesson which requires that the United States and its allies develop a full spectrum of military strength, under sensitive and flexible control, capable of covering all regions of the free world, if we are to create a stable military environment and minimize the opportunity for Communist intrusions.

It is toward this objective that we have been working over the past three years. We have been building American military forces over the whole range from virtually unattackable Polaris submarines to the training of our own men and the soldiers of our allies to deter or to defeat guerrilla warfare.

We have made it clear to those who might attack that a nuclear assault on ourselves or our allies would bring in return nuclear disaster. We have made it clear that we would use all the force at our disposal if we or our allies are attacked massively by other means; but we require also the kinds of force that would permit us to deter or deal with limited Communist attack without having to choose between nuclear war and surrender.

At the same time we recognize that the arms race is an unsatisfactory way to provide national security in a nuclear age. We are prepared to take either limited or radical evenhanded measures to reduce the risks of war and the burden of armaments, so long as we are confident that these measures can be verified and controlled by effective measures of inspection. This has been the burden of our position at the Geneva Disarmament Conference.

Our approach to problems of arms control and disarmament is not in terms of propaganda; it is a soberly weighed aspect of national security policy. We are in deadly earnest. But no amount of United States staff work or seriousness of intent can substitute for the essential missing ingredient: a Soviet willingness to acknowledge and to act on the simple fact that an end to the arms race requires a progressive opening of societies to mutual inspection.

The fifth element in our strategy concerns our posture toward the nations now under Communist rule. We have made it clear that we do not intend to initiate nuclear war to destroy the Communist world. The question then arises: Are we content merely to fend off Communist intrusion, military and subversive? What are our hopes and our prospects with respect to the Communist world? Are we reconciled to a planet that shall, at best, be forever split?

We are engaged in an historic test of strength—not merely of military strength but of our capacity to understand and to deal with the forces at work in the world about us. The ultimate question at issue is whether this small planet is to be organized on the principles of the Communist bloc or on the principles of voluntary cooperation among independent nation-states dedicated to human freedom. If we succeed in defending the present frontiers of freedom, the outcome of that test of strength will be determined by slow moving forces of history. It will be determined by whether the elements in the world environment, which I listed earlier, are more successfully gripped and organized by ourselves and our friends than by the Communists.

The question then becomes: How is history moving? Are these underlying forces now working for us or against us?

I would put it to you strongly that they are working our way, if we have the wit to work with them.

First, in the more industrialized North we have seen in the postwar years a remarkable demonstration which has had a more profound effect on Communist thought than is generally understood. Until very recently the Communists believed that the United States was something of a special case. We were viewed as the fortunate democratic island-continent with much land and few people, permitted to enjoy—at least for a time—a special favored destiny. They looked to Europe and Japan as more vulnerable regions subject to Communist takeover in the fairly near future. What has been demonstrated in the past decade is that advanced democratic societies have learned to avoid protracted phases of severe unemployment and that the American pattern of development—our standard of living and the provision of high standards of consumption to the mass of the people—is the general pattern. The trend toward the Americanization of standards of living in Western Europe and Japan, and the vitality of democratic capitalism in the past decade, is a major setback to the Communist image of history, to their ideology, and to their working plans.

Partly because of this setback they have looked with increasing hope and enterprise to the underdeveloped areas. There they thought the Communist methods of organization and the Communist example in China, North Vietnam, and elsewhere—as a means of moving an underdeveloped country forward rapidly toward modern status—would draw others to the bloc. They turned to a strategy of outflanking and isolating the United States, Europe, and Japan by winning over the underdeveloped areas—by ideological attraction as well as by subversion, aid, and diplomacy.

The returns are not yet in; but a sober and cautious assessment shows this: Where the Communists have had power in underdeveloped areas—in China, North Korea, North Vietnam, and now in Cuba—they have done an unimpressive job technically, quite aside from the inhumanity of a police state. The most striking fact about the mood in Asia, when I went out there with General Taylor in 1961, was the loss by the Communists of their power to attract by example in either North Vietnam or in China. The Communist states are drab and hungry. In particular, the Chinese Communists have demonstrated that the most powerful control machine ever mounted in an underdeveloped country is incapable of forcing men to grow enough food; and their agricultural crisis has compounded into a general crisis of industrial production and foreign exchange.

Meanwhile, India and certain other underdeveloped nations have begun to demonstrate that real momentum and steady progress can be obtained in an underdeveloped area by mobilizing the energies and loyalties of the people by consent and normal human incentives.

The demonstration in the underdeveloped areas is not yet as definitive a victory for freedom as that in the northern half of the free world. One of the great tasks of this decade is to complete this demonstration. But the lesson of our experience thus far is that we should be confident that in going forward with economic development by the methods of pragmatic planning and individual consent which are natural to us, we are on the right track technically as well as morally; and that the Communist image of the problems of modernization—and Communist techniques for handling them in the underdeveloped areas—are just as archaic as their notions of how one should organize an advanced industrial society.

There is yet another force working our way, and that is the intent of people and governments in the underdeveloped areas to maintain their independence.

The drive for independence is a most powerful force. We can honestly align our policy with this force. In the end the Communists cannot, and this is one fundamental reason why the Communist offensive in the underdeveloped areas will fail.

Finally, the Communist bloc itself is now in the midst of a slow-moving but great historical crisis. This crisis takes the form of the deep dispute between Moscow and Peiping—a dispute which has engaged, in one way or another, Communist parties throughout the world. What lies behind this dispute, among other factors, is the rise of nationalism as a living and growing force within the Communist bloc. It is a force within Russia itself, and it is a growing force in other regions where Communist regimes are in power. Despite the interest of Communists in maintaining their cohesion against the West, the slow fragmentation of the Communist bloc and the diffusion of power within it go forward.

We expect no quick or cheap benefits from this process. In the short run it may present problems to us, as when the Russians and the Chinese compete to exert their influence over the Communist party in Hanoi. But, fundamentally, the assertion of nationalism and national interests within the Communist bloc should tend to produce a more livable world. The diffusion of power, we know, is the basis for human liberty within societies; and on the world scene it is the basis for independent nations.

For example, we have every reason to believe that the limited assistance we have given Yugoslavia and Poland over the years and our willingness to maintain wide human contacts with their citizens have been sound long-run investments in the principle of national independence and human freedom.

We should, therefore, be prepared—as these national interests exert themselves—to find limited areas of overlapping interest with Communist regimes and to work toward a world which increasingly approximates the kind of world we envisaged when the United Nations was set up.

Our strategy is, then, quite simple. We are working from day to day to bind up in closer partnership the industrialized nations of the north, to work with our friends in the north to create a new partnership between the more developed and less developed nations. Recognizing and welcoming the new strength to be found in Western Europe and Japan, recognizing and welcoming the impulse of the southern nations to modernize, we see a path ahead which would reconcile the great interests involved and gradually build a community of free nations.

We intend to defend this community of free nations and to do so in ways which will minimize the possibility that a nuclear war will come about; and we intend—with all the poise and insight we can muster—to draw the nations now under Communist regimes toward the free world community by both ruling out the expansion of communism and exploiting specific areas of overlapping interest which we believe will increasingly emerge as the strength, unity, and effectiveness of the free community is demonstrated. As Secretary Rusk has said: ". . . we should be aware that the concepts of independent nationhood, of national interest and of natural culture, are day to day asserting themselves strongly" within the Communist bloc. We have every reason to be confident that the wave of the future lies with the fundamental principles on which our own society is based and which are rooted also in the United Nations Charter.

It is in this spirit—in terms of these objectives and this intent—that we do our work from day to day in Washington. We know that there will be frustrations and setbacks. We know that we shall have to deal with difficult crises as well as press forward with our work of construction. But, as we go about our business, we are in good heart, and we shall not be deflected. We believe that time is on the side of the things this nation stands for, if we use time well; and we intend to do so.

III *Power and Diplomacy*

We stand, as I write, in the midst of a relatively quiet interval in the cold war, as compared to the period January 1961–October 1962, when the Berlin, Southeast Asian, Congolese, and Cuban crises were in a more acute stage. While it is a virtually universal hope that this relatively quiet interval will lead on to more substantial movement toward a stable peace, that outcome is by no means certain. We could evidently lapse back to acute crisis; or the present uneasy situation could persist for some time.

It is, therefore, a good moment to look back at the principles that have guided us in recent years, when the nation's central task on the world scene was to turn back Khrushchev's post-Sputnik offensive, if possible without major military engagement. That exercise—on the whole successful—was rooted in certain basic concepts governing national security policy.

At the heart of national security policy in the contemporary world is the relation between military and nonmilitary objectives, between force and politics. We start with two propositions:

First, there is hardly a diplomatic relationship we conduct that is not colored by an assessment of United States military power and by the circumstances in which we are likely to bring it into play. Our military capabilities and our will to use them in the pursuit of vital national interests and purposes are the inescapable backdrop for the whole of our civil policy.

Second, our objectives are, in the largest sense, political, not military. We regard ourselves as engaged in a fundamental, historical contest as to how the community of nations shall be organized; whether it shall be on the basis of a Communist empire and Communist police-state dictatorships, or on the basis of independent nations which act together—out of a spontaneous recognition of their areas of interdependence—and move progressively toward higher degrees of human freedom.

As the Secretary of State has said, our goal is victory. He went on to explain: "One hears now and then that we have a 'no win' purpose or policies. That is simply not so. Of course we intend to win. And we are going to win. Our objective is a victory for all mankind.

"For let us be clear about what we mean when we say, 'We are going to win.' Who makes up the 'we'? Not only 185 million Americans, but most of the rest of the people of the world. And what is the worldwide victory we work for? Not the victory of one nation over another or of one people over another, but a worldwide victory for freedom. . . ."

A military policy which is an effective servant of this grand objective must begin with an appreciation of three fundamental facts.

First, the Soviet Union now commands sufficient nuclear power and delivery capability to inflict enormous destruction on Western Europe, and great and increasing destruction on the United States. It is, therefore, part of national policy to pursue our purposes by means that minimize the likelihood of nuclear war, while recognizing that it is always possible and must be contemplated in defense of our vital interests.

Second, it has been, thus far, Communist policy to avoid general nuclear war with the United States, which would result in massive damage to societies under Communist control and, indeed, gravely risk the continuity of that control. In fact, from 1945 to the present, Communist policy has systematically avoided confrontation with United States points of real strength.

Third, Communist thrusts into the free world have been

based on a combination of political pressure designed to exploit the free world's fear of nuclear war and upon limited probes against particular areas and types of free world vulnerability.

Looking back to 1945, one can quite easily reconstruct the thinking of Communist planners. They systematically chose their directions of thrust after a careful analysis of gaps in the free world spectrum of defense. Regionally, for example, they probed northern Azerbaijan, Greece, Berlin, Indochina, and South Korea. In general, they have been acutely aware of the vulnerability of the free world to techniques of subversion and guerrilla warfare which, until recently, appeared to lie beneath the threshold of our effective defensive capabilities.

Faced with this kind of enemy, a rational military policy must include these elements:

First, the maintenance of a sophisticated mix of delivery vehicles for nuclear weapons, so dispersed, hardened, mobile, and controlled that the U.S.S.R. could not count with confidence, despite any technological breakthrough it might reasonably expect to achieve, upon neutralizing or blunting a large proportion of United States retaliatory power; and which would permit us, even after an initial Soviet surprise attack, to inflict unacceptable civil and military damage upon the enemy. We require this capability because Communist planners must never be able to see profit in any form of nuclear encounter or any confrontation which might lead to it.

Second, we require a full spectrum of general purpose forces and counterguerrilla forces sufficient to make nonnuclear aggression into the free world increasingly unpromising to the Communists, and permit us to frustrate such aggression without being forced by nonnuclear weakness to resort to nuclear weapons.

In broadest terms, the military objective is to create from these instruments an environment which will permit us to achieve maximum deterrence of deliberate aggression, and especially aggression with nuclear weapons; to minimize the likelihood of uncalculated, unpremeditated, or unintended nuclear conflicts, and to deal successfully with aggression in such ways that the intensity of conflict is controlled, enemy escalation is deterred, and general war does not result from the uncontrolled pressures of crises and limited conflicts.

We seek, in short, a military environment of maximum stability consistent with our national interests and purposes.

These conventional and laborious phrases are by no means abstract, bureaucratic boiler plate. They are working guides for our government as we face specific day-to-day tasks of leading the free world in the cold war.

Think for a moment of how the Cuban crisis of October 1962 was conducted. The Soviet Union sought to shift the political and military balance of power on the world scene at a stroke. If we had accepted the missiles in Cuba—beneath our early warning network—our nuclear capability would have been substantially degraded; the credibility in Moscow and in Europe of our commitment to West Berlin would have been put in grave question; the image of Soviet power would have been projected starkly into Latin America; and the expectation of further extension of Soviet power in Latin America, and other underdeveloped areas, would have radically increased.

From the Soviet point of view, this was a limited thrust whose success depended on these three elements: first, the shadow over the West of Soviet nuclear power; second, the likelihood of a political split within the West as to whether the issue in Cuba was worth the risk of nuclear war; and third, the likelihood that the United States, in the face of these dangers and schisms, would not be prepared to initiate—I repeat, to initiate—military action.

President Kennedy's response—worked out under the pressure of a unique crisis—closely followed the general lines of basic policy which had evolved within his administration. He defined a clear and limited political objective: the removal from Cuba of offensive weapons. He rallied to this policy our allies in Latin America, a prior basis having been created by careful diplomacy over many months. The Atlantic Community as well rallied around, partly as a result of allied solidarity, partly out of appreciation that this was a crucial United States–U.S.S.R. confrontation and not merely a matter of United States distaste for Castro.

President Kennedy chose a form of initiative which was limited but directly relevant to the political objective: a discriminating quarantine. Behind this limited move, we commanded, in an advanced state of alert, a very wide range of general purpose and nuclear forces capable of dealing with any level of escalation that Moscow might select in response to our initiative.

Essential to this exercise was a simple fact: There was not an ounce of bluff in the American position. As a government and as a nation, we were deadly serious about a deadly serious matter.

The limited initial action chosen by President Kennedy gave the Soviet authorities an opportunity to realize that they had miscalculated and to reverse their course. But, if our limited initial action had not been effectively persuasive, we would have taken further steps. We were determined to eliminate Soviet offensive weapons from this hemisphere and prepared to do whatever was necessary to achieve that end.

In a preliminary assessment of the lessons of the Cuban crisis, the inextricable connection between military force and diplomacy is plain. On the one hand, the whole exercise hinged on the existence of a full range of appropriate United States military capabilities and the evident will to use them if necessary. On the other hand, our use of force, or threat to use it, was related to a limited, legal, and lucidly defined objective: the unacceptability in this hemisphere of Soviet offensive weapons. In this crisis, there was no diplomatic move which did not have a military component, and there was no military move which was not related intimately to our diplomatic and political requirements and purposes.

Just as Moscow's adventure with offensive weapons in Cuba, if successful, would have had world-wide military and nonmilitary consequences—affecting the whole balance of the cold war—so its withdrawal of those weapons has had substantial costs to the international Communist movement, the full measure of which is still unfolding.

The Cuban crisis was the most intense and dangerous of the politico-military crises of the past two years, but it was only one of several. In Laos, for example, President Kennedy set a political objective: the creation of a neutral, independent Laos. But movement toward that objective was not achieved by diplomatic means alone. Twice in the course of these difficult—and still unfinished—negotiations, the Communists tested our military capabilities and will. In May 1961, the President was forced to decide to put forces into the Mekong Valley if a ceasefire was not promptly agreed on; and in April 1962, after the fall of Nam Tha, some five thousand Marines and Army personnel, installed in Thailand, cooled off a potentially dangerous Pathet Lao offensive.

In Vietnam, we are committed to maintain the political independence of South Vietnam in the face of the guerrilla war mounted, in its present phase, from Hanoi since 1958. To achieve this political result has required that we radically increase the American military presence there, but it is too soon to say whether or not it will be necessary for us to signal that we are prepared to apply more force in order to achieve our objective—and to mean it.

The military initiatives with respect to Laos and Vietnam, in pursuit of clearly defined and limited political objectives, would have had no serious effect on the course of events unless the Communist leaders concerned were convinced that echeloned behind these limited demonstrations of force there were both the capabilities and the will to deal with every form of escalation they might mount in response, up to and including all-out nuclear war.

In the Congo, we experienced in 1961–1962 an even more complex politico-military exercise. Our objective was to help create an independent and unified nation in the Congo. That objective was endangered by the evident Communist ambition to establish a base in Central Africa, which would have provided exceedingly attractive possibilities for subversion and guerrilla warfare throughout the region.

In this case, the military force actually involved was mounted by the United Nations, without calling on the troops, if any, of the major powers. Every inch of the way has been difficult. But the danger of the installation of a Communist-controlled government has been thus far forestalled by a combination of awkward, interminable, frustrating—but quite effective—military and political moves.

The greatest and most difficult of the exercises in politico-military operations thus far undertaken has been in Berlin, where the immediate tactical situation is by no means as favorable to us as it is in the Caribbean, or even in Southeast Asia, and where the possibilities of the controlled use of force and diplomacy appear, at first glance, to be narrower.

Nevertheless, contingency planning has proceeded in line with the principles I have outlined. We and our allies have set a clear political objective: the maintenance of West Berlin as a vital city, living in freedom, its access to the West unencumbered and protected by the presence of Western forces. We have planned to maintain those vital interests of the West by the application, if necessary, of measured, but always sufficient, counterforce, against the background of President Kennedy's commitment of July 1961 that we would go to nuclear war, if necessary, to defend West Berlin.

The interweaving of military and nonmilitary action in these five crises has not been confined to what might be called the framework of confrontation with the Communist powers. The linkage has been even more intimate. In the case of Cuba, we have been concerned with the state of mind of the peoples of Latin America as well as of their leaders, with the psychological and political consequences of our policy in Cuba itself, with the impact of the crisis on our NATO allies, and with the very special politics of the United Nations.

In Vietnam and Laos, the nature of the defense problem has required an extraordinary intimacy and common understanding—both in the field and in Washington—of the interconnections between political, economic, and military policy. That interconnection is of the essence of guerilla warfare. It was a judgment by the Vietnamese military that the politics of Diem's regime was incompatible with victory against the Communists which, essentially, caused the coup of October 2, 1963.

In Berlin, our military and civil authorities have been concerned not merely with the defense of our vital interests, but also with the morale of the Berliners and the problem of that city's long-run economic and psychological health and vigor in the face of the Wall. This concern has not only weighed in military decisons, as in the case of our rapid reinforcement in 1961, but has led to a major viability program, covering economic, cultural, and political affairs in the city which had led not merely to a stabilization of the city's population but a net flow to West Berlin of young and talented Germans.

If one looks back at this history of the cold war since 1945, there is nothing very new about the exercises I have just cited. We have been living for the past seventeen years in a world of limited clashes of force—limited in immediate objectives, in terrain, and in weapons—each intimately interwoven with diplomacy and politics. We responded to limited Communist probes with limited means: in Greece, the Berlin blockade of 1948–

1949, Korea, Quemoy-Matsu, and other points of confrontation.

Since then there have been two significant developments. First, our basic national security policy now accepts the central reality of this type of controlled, limited, politico-military confrontation. These episodes are not regarded as exceptions to the rule, to be dealt with *ad hoc,* but as the form the struggle is most likely to assume. Moreover, it is judged that we have a better chance to deter such Communist probes if we develop *before* the event a full spectrum of capabilities—nuclear, conventional, and counterinsurgent. With respect to problems of counterinsurgency, our objective is to defeat the Communists in the initial stage of their efforts to gain power—when they are building the political foundations for insurrection and before full-fledged guerrilla war (of the Vietnam type) can be mounted.

The second difference lies in the expanding Soviet nuclear delivery capabilities. Here there has been a fundamental question that the United States in particular, and the West, in general, had to answer if there was to be any hope of a stable military environment.

It has been basic to Khrushchev's stance on the world scene—at least since his evocation of nuclear blackmail in April 1956—that the West might accept limited setbacks rather than risk a direct confrontation and nuclear war, once Moscow acquired fusion weapons and rockets. It is evident that his policies with respect to Berlin and, later, with respect to the installation of offensive weapons in Cuba, were strongly colored by this hope. The question, then, was this: Would the United States be willing, in the new nuclear environment, to act in defense of vital Western interests with the strength and will that it had exhibited in earlier times when the Soviet nuclear threat was less substantial. This was a question being asked not merely in Moscow but in every other capital.

I remember well a conversation, in July, 1961, with a Soviet diplomat. He stated his belief that, under the strain of a Berlin crisis, none of our European allies would continue to support the position in West Berlin. I then pointed out to him that Hitler had made a similar misjudgment about the British in the 1930s at a time when, superficially, they did not appear united, strong, and determined. He immediately replied: "That was before nuclear weapons existed." I suggested that if you back men against the wall with nuclear weapons, although it might not make sense statistically or historically, they were likely to behave on the principle: "I can only die once."

In a sense, the men in Moscow have had to establish whether the nerve and will of the West matched their own. This is the essence of the problem of credibility. The whole Communist movement has been, since its origins, rooted in the conviction that the disciplined conspiratorial minority who form the core of Communist organization can overwhelm the greater potential power of non-Communists by their greater purposefulness and toughness of fiber. Behind all the elaborate mechanisms of diplomacy, behind the incredible complexity and sophistication of the world of nuclear weapons and delivery vehicles, the cold war comes down to this test of whether we and the democratic world are fundamentally tougher and more purposeful in the defense of our vital interests than they are in the pursuit of their global ambitions.

One would hope that it is now understood, after the crises of the past several years, that the American people, as well as their government, accept the fact that the heart of a credible deterrent in a nuclear age lies in being prepared to face the consequences, should deterrence fail.

Current national security policy, then, is not basically new. It builds on how four postwar United States administrations have faced their responsibilities in protecting the frontiers of freedom. But it also aims to make less attractive to Moscow and Peking the kind of Communist enterprises which, for example, between 1958 and 1961 placed Southeast Asia, Central Africa, and the Caribbean—as well as West Berlin—in mortal danger.

For its execution, such a policy requires that the military and civil arms of government work together in the greatest intimacy and mutual respect. The progress made in this direction over recent years has been substantial, as a new generation of military men and civilians has emerged whose mature experience has been dominated by the curious struggle of politics and force which is the cold war.

IV Ideas and Action

Many of us who now work in Washington were too young to have been caught up in the challenge of the depression years and the New Deal period. We were formed by the second world war; after 1945 we were drawn to a continuing concern with the problems of this nation's position on the world scene. Along with many others of my age, my professional life has been a counterpoint between the world of ideas and the world of public policy: In my case, the emphasis has been on military and foreign policy. Of the years since 1940, for example, I spent eleven in public service, thirteen in universities, with a good portion of the latter involving consultation in Washington. The proportions are quite typical. Those of us now in our forties, then, are in a sense children of the era that began with the fall of Paris in 1940 and that has continued through the two decades of world responsibility for the United States which followed that tragic June day.

I am by profession an historian and an economist; so my theoretical prism is that of the social scientist. The intellectual problems to which the social scientist has addressed himself over the past twenty years have been shaped by America's emerging world role to a degree which matches the extent to which science and engineering have been drawn into the challenges of weaponry and space.

For this, neither the social scientist nor the natural scientist need apologize. We have not forsaken the long tradition of Western intellectual life. Many of the fundamental theoretical achievements of the natural sciences have resulted from efforts to solve practical problems—from the flow of the Nile in the ancient world to the requirements of navigation in the fifteenth and sixteenth centuries, down to the contemporary struggle to understand and to defeat the viruses.

In the social sciences most of the great theoretical works—from Aristotle to Keynes—have also been, in part, pamphlets for the times.

This is not to say that all natural scientists should attempt to solve engineering or medical problems—or that all fruitful work in the social sciences should incorporate recommendations for public policy. The world of ideas is a spacious world. It has place within it for all manner of talents and tastes: for those who find satisfaction ordering narrow areas of fact, as well as for those who are concerned with the grand design; for those who find in the world of ideas a pure aesthetic satisfaction as well as those who strain to extract from it practical lessons for the society of which they are a part and the human beings with whom they share a generation.

Moreover, the world of science, whatever its relevance to the affairs of the day, should have a continuity and pride of its own —to a degree, withdrawn, protected, and, if necessary, defiant of the active world.

In the end, however, a rude pragmatism shapes the content of intellectual life; and, in turn, the behavior of practical men is governed by the abstractions which men of ideas have created in an effort to give a degree of order to the world of human beings and things about them.

As Santayana said: "Practical men may not notice it, but in fact human discourse is intrinsically addressed not to natural existing things but to ideal essences, poetic or logical terms which thought may define and play with. When fortune or necessity diverts our attention from this congenial sport to crude facts and pressing issues, we turn our frail poetic ideas into symbols for those terrible irruptive things. In that paper money of our own stamping, the legal tender of the mind, we are obliged to reckon all the movements and values of the world."

We live at a time when the fate of our society—its ability to understand and control its environment, indeed, its ability to survive—is closely linked to the relationship which Santayana described. In the most practical and concrete sense, our ability to bring to bear on the "crude facts and pressing issues" the appropriate "legal tender of the mind" will determine whether our kind of society can maintain for itself a world environment which will permit it to continue to develop in continuity with our historic past. It was one thing to build a humane democracy on an empty continent, protected from the struggles for world power; it is a quite different matter to maintain it in a world of nuclear weapons and missiles at a time when the protection of the whole free world against the dour and purposeful thrust of the Communist bloc comes instantly to rest on the American people.

The linkage between ideas and action is most obvious, of course, in the making of military policy and in contriving the instruments which will make it effective in a world of modern science and technology. The competitive arms race in which we are engaged reaches out into every field of science and engineering. The era of missiles and nuclear weapons has shaped—where it has not dominated—physics, electronics, chemistry, and the development of materials, as well as many other fields from meteorology to oceanography.

But more is involved here than merely the construction in good time of the appropriate weapons and forces required to deter aggression. The protection of the frontiers of freedom in ways which minimize the likelihood of a nuclear war is a most searching political and psychological—as well as scientific, engineering, and production—enterprise. We are engaged in a relentless struggle with the Communist powers in which our strength and theirs, our vital interests and theirs, our diplomacy and theirs, the viability of free world societies and theirs, are endlessly at play.

There is hardly a diplomatic relationship we conduct in the world, or move that we make, that does not involve within it the question: Does the United States have the capacity and the will to use military force to back its play?

For that reason there is no posture which is more likely to lead to nuclear war than the notion that nuclear war is unthinkable. If nuclear war were unthinkable, there would be no limit to the temptations of those who are committed to the dangerous but illusory idea that world power is an attainable goal; and if they were thus led to overplay their hand, we would have to react late and convulsively.

At every stage, then, the protection of the free world from aggression by means which minimize the likelihood of nuclear war is a searching test not merely of the capacity of our society to develop the right kind of weapons in the right sequence but of the ability of our society and its allies and friends so to conduct themselves as to make aggression in any form unattractive and to deal with aggression when it occurs in ways which minimize the likelihood that the ultimate sanction of nuclear strength would have to be invoked.

This is a subtle and difficult business. But those who bear responsibility in our government and, in the end, all of our people must understand its dimensions and accept it with coolness and poise. It requires an effort of imagination—an ability to translate hypothetical future situations into current action—into things as palpable as a new missile or an outgoing cable. We must live with abstract projections into the future as if they were today's headlines; for the lead times of modern technology and modern communications give little time to learn on the job.

This task requires a frame of mind very different from

Tocqueville's vision of Americans as simple empiricists immersing themselves in the palpable immediate tasks of organizing a continental society and making it work. In military affairs we have historically been unprepared when conflict began, only then turning to the task of learning what the war was about, what it required of men and of arms. In the first and second world wars our power was only coming to a peak as the wars came to an end. Time, distance, and allies made this a possible posture for the United States, although costly to the world at large and to ourselves. The relevant time is now reduced to hours, if not minutes; distance has shrunk so that we now stand in the front line; and there are no allies to buy us time to mobilize and to learn. We must, therefore, steadily behave in ways which persuade a potential enemy that war is unprofitable; and, as a result, the intellectual content of military policy—the role of ideas and of the ability to act on ideas—becomes critical. And this is, of course, equally the case with that aspect of military policy which consists of the field of arms control and disarmament; for if we are to make progress in this area—as we must over the long pull—it will come about not from wishful hopes, but from hardheaded creation, involving scientific, military, and political thought, combined, at last, with a Soviet acceptance of effective international inspection.

What is true of military and arms control policy is true in a different way of our relations with the various regions and peoples of the globe.

The interests of nations are now so sensitively interwoven and communications are so quick and ample that conventional diplomacy no longer describes how the world works. Our allies in Europe, for example, who depend on our military strength for their security, and will do so for the foreseeable future, are as sensitive to the moods and nuances of American politics as any American. An ambiguous phrase, a misinterpreted background conference, an imagined line of policy deduced from some action we take—these produce reactions which are much more like the interplay of politics within a given nation than the formal discourses of classic diplomacy.

More than that, we are caught up with our European friends —and also with Japan and the countries of the British Commonwealth—in a period of extraordinary structural change in the world's arrangements. Everywhere old relationships are changing and new ones are being forged. Everywhere nations are redefining where they stand on the world scene, what their relations to their neighbors and to the whole community of nations will be. The changes involved in the forging of a new transatlantic partnership go deep into the history of each nation concerned, to their view of themselves and of the future. For Americans to play a constructive role in this exciting new phase of history requires of us a sympathetic knowledge of other people's history, of their perspectives, their fears, and their ambitions more profound than any required of us in the past. We cannot rely here—any more than we can in military policy—on simple, pragmatic learning-on-the-job or a projection to others of attitudes instinctive to us. We must reach out and understand the minds of many peoples if this great job of architecture, in which we are engaged with our friends, is to be sound and stand the tests and strains of time.

Even more difficult, perhaps, is the task of creating and bringing to bear the ideas and actions which will relate us to the nations, mainly in the southern half of the globe, which are now caught up in the adventure of modernizing their societies—nations new and old, in Asia, the Middle East, Africa, and Latin America. They are in stages of development which we knew in our own experience a century or more ago. Moreover, they are learning how to organize themselves for growth and are beginning to grow in settings very different from those of early nineteenth century America. Not only do they lack the special blessing that we had—of much good land and relatively few people—but they come to these tasks out of historical and cultural settings very different from those of the United States.

Nevertheless, if we are to maintain for our own society a world environment which will permit us to develop in continuity with our past, we must understand these distant societies and understand them with sufficient insight and sympathy so that we can work in partnership with the men and women, as well as the governments, they contain.

This is a difficult job. It requires that we develop concepts of economic, social, and political development which transcend our own experience and embrace their problems.

But it is not an impossible job; and it is made easier because, in the end, we Americans cannot resist supporting the disadvantaged and we find it difficult to keep out of great constructive ventures. It is made easier, also because behind the particular problems of the new nations and the special settings in which they occur are universal and recognizable human impulses—for the dignity of their nations and the welfare of their children.

Nevertheless, to formulate and execute policies which will link the more developed and less developed nations of the free world requires of us a marriage of ideas and action as challenging as that required to conduct a rational military policy in a world of nuclear weapons.

But that is not all. If the great struggle in which we are engaged on the world scene is to be resolved without war, it must be resolved on the basis of historical processes of peaceful change. Rarely in history has any group of men more plainly articulated their hostile objectives than the Communist leadership in stating their intentions toward the free world. If we are not prepared for any form of aggression—from nuclear war to guerrillas in the rice paddies—it is not the fault of our opponents. On the other hand, it is not enough for us to regard them merely as a hostile force. History has not stopped within the Communist bloc. There are forces at work making for change.

Moreover, the simple vision of Marx and Lenin did not prepare the Communist leadership for a world of nuclear weapons and of resurgent nationalism on both sides of the Iron Curtain; or for a system of democratic capitalism which has exhibited a remarkable resilience and capacity for adaptation. Nor did it prepare them to grow food efficiently or to cope with generations of the young who, looking about in the dim bureaucratic world of a police state, set aside the slogans, examine the world about them as it really is, and commit themselves to the search for answers to the oldest and most basic human questions—the meaning of life and how the integrity and uniqueness of the individual should find expression in a complex society.

And so there is thrust on us not merely the requirement of defending a free world community in an age of modern technology, not merely the task of weaving together its more developed and less developed regions, but also the need to understand with insight the forces at work in Communist societies and the duty to encourage the development of areas—even limited areas—of overlapping interest.

In the end, then, the making of public policy in the times in which we live is a most searching task in engineering. We must bring to bear on our environment in a unified way all that both the natural and social sciences can teach us, and we must do so in settings which cannot be read out automatically from either the social or technological life of contemporary America.

It is a fair question to ask whether the intellectual and philosophical traditions of our nation and its educational institutions are capable of producing men who can cope with this searching test—who can both generate the appropriate ideas and put them into action. I believe, quite soberly, that we have cause for confidence. Just as a century ago in the Morrill Act we launched a set of institutions which could serve our society at a time when we needed improved agricultural technology and railway, mining, and industrial engineers, our contemporary institutions have responded in a remarkable way to the current requirements of our society.

But whatever new intellectual and operational virtuosity we develop, it is essential that we retain certain old American virtues: above all the conviction that, within limits, the future can be shaped, that problems can be solved, and that, with strength, patience, and insight, the long tradition of which we are a part shall continue to be the mainstream of human history, to be joined by non-Western streams which essentially share its humane ethic.

Our nation was born out of a commitment to ideas—incorporated in the Declaration of Independence and the Constitution—which transcend our own borders. There has never been a time—not even at the height of the second world war—when this commitment has been more real or required of us more loyalty.

We who now bear a measure of responsibility in Washington are building on all those who have gone before. Where we have moved correctly, we have learned from past successes and failures.

There are those, viewing the tensions and weapons of our times, the environment of revolution in the world about us, who hanker for quieter days, who look with nostalgia to a past when the world environment of our society was less dangerous and the challenges to us less severe. But we cannot renounce our destiny. We are the trustees of the principles of national independence and human freedom all over the globe; and, given our history, this is a proud and natural responsibility.

We are challenged—as controller of the greatest military force the world has ever seen—to see this planet safely through these times until the day when nuclear weapons are brought under effective international discipline and control.

We are challenged at home to maintain and develop this society as a solid base for our world position—and this challenge comes to rest on our scientists and engineers, our business and labor leaders, our school boards—in fact, it comes to rest on every citizen.

It was never promised to men that life would be without risk, and we Americans have achieved nothing on this continent without effort and danger.

Part II

The Atlantic Community: Problems of the North

V *The Atlantic Community: An American View*

Both the problems and the possibilities of the Atlantic Alliance are best viewed in a long perspective. For, the Atlantic Alliance is not a new concept. It has come to its present stage after almost a generation's hard work on both sides of the Atlantic.

In recalling the evolution of our policies it is, perhaps, wholesome for an American to begin by acknowledging how badly our diplomacy toward Europe performed between the two world wars.

By failing to join the League of Nations and by failing to meet the French desire for an unambiguous long-term American security commitment to the European continent, the United States set the framework for the interwar tragedy of Europe. And elements in European diplomacy also left Paris without steady support and failed to build a policy which would maintain the viability and independence of the new states of Eastern Europe and support those in Germany who wished to pursue a moderate and constructive course.

In the end, of course, our perhaps retrievable errors of the 1920s were rendered disastrous by the Great Depression which drained away a good part of the energy and capacity of the West to pursue effective policies on the world scene; and so we had to fight what Churchill has properly designated an unnecessary war.

I recall these events—at once distant and part of our lives—because on the American side our policy toward Europe and the Atlantic community has been colored by an assessment of where and how we failed in an earlier generation. It was a notable feature of American policy during the second world war that President Roosevelt was almost obsessively concerned to ensure that, this time, the United States would have the political base to enter the new world organization that succeeded the League of Nations. And from 1946 forward our approach to European problems has been strongly colored by the need to avoid the kinds of mistakes we had made earlier, as we interpreted them, notably with respect to the European continent.

As it became clear in the winter and spring of 1946 that the Soviet Union would not permit the unification of Germany on the basis of political freedom, we began to shape a policy that still stands; namely, a policy of helping to build a prosperous and united Western Europe which would be closely linked in military and other great affairs to the United States and Canada, and which would move back onto the world scene as a great power, broadly in concert with North America.

Four elements converged to produce this policy.

First, there was Germany. It was judged essential that we create a strong, unified European structure which could receive as an equal partner a Germany that was bound to be split for some time to come, a structure which would give to Germans an opportunity to mobilize their great energy and resources along constructive lines in the face of the inevitable strains that history and geography have placed upon them.

Second, there was Moscow. Europe faced a unified adversary consolidating his empire up to the Elbe, seeking to exploit every schism or lesion he could find in the West. A united Europe linked to the United States appeared the only tolerably safe framework of organization to deal with this centralized, increasingly powerful locus of active hostility.

Third, there was the perception to which many men had come on both sides of the Atlantic as the major historic lesson of the second world war; namely, that in the world of the second half of the twentieth century the individual nation-states of Europe could only execute effectively a major role on the world scene if they were to unite. The arena of world affairs had widened out to embrace the whole of the planet, and the technology of effective power had outstripped the scale of the old states of Europe. The historic competition for power and status among them could only be pursued at the cost of their common effectiveness as a voice in world affairs, as well as at the risk of their common security.

And, finally, there was the economic argument: The full economic potentialities of Europe could only be developed on the basis of a spacious, highly competitive continental market.

As a minor official in the Department of State when these matters were first debated, early in 1946, I can recall vividly that the dangers of this policy for the United States were laid on the table: How could we be sure that a united Europe would, in fact, pursue policies consonant with American interests? Would it not be safer to conduct a bilateral set of relations with Europe which, given the potentialities of our bargaining power, might permit us to assure United States influence in European affairs over a longer period?

We decided that the larger interests should prevail. And in the Marshall Plan and beyond we went forward in support of European unity. Behind this decision was an act of faith—faith that the ultimate logic of the Atlantic connection, already tested in two world wars and then under a third test by Stalin, would prevail; and that a united Europe would build its policy on the fundamental overlaps in our respective interests, not on the potential cross purposes and divergencies—which were, and are, evident enough.

We have never looked back on that decision, and we are confident at the present time and in the face of contemporary problems and difficulties that it remains the right basis for American policy.

It is also true, however, that we are now in the midst of a decade which will test whether that policy is, in fact, viable.

We are in the midst of the most complex and delicate piece of international architecture ever undertaken at a time of peace; namely, the transition in the relations between Europe and the United States from dependence to partnership, and a simultaneous realignment in the relations of the European states to one another, centered on the question of European unity.

The fact is, of course, that in the postwar years the United States had to pick up around the world one area of responsibility after another, either to fill vacuums left by the second world war—as in Korea and Japan—or to cope with situations where the European powers withdrew. If one examines the map in the vast arc from, say, Korea to Greece, and observes where American fighting men, money, and political commitments are emplaced, at every point it is clear we moved in to fill a gap which would otherwise have been filled by chaos or the Communists.

It is our hope and expectation that this abnormal preponderance of the American role in Asia, the Middle East, and Africa—and I would add, in Latin America—will give place to a new balance. Europe has the resources, the latent energy and, if it unites, I believe the political energy and will to return to the world scene on a new basis.

We do not regard the relationships which grew up *ad hoc* after the second world war between the United States and these regions as a final or appropriate pattern. We look toward the emergence of a general relationship of the more advanced nations of the northern part of the free world with the developing nations to the south in which the role of Europe and Japan relative to the United States would gradually expand. We believe this return of Europe and Japan to the world scene would be good for the United States, good for Europe and Japan, and good for the nations and regions now caught up in the adventure of modernizing their societies.

This vision poses for the Atlantic Alliance a question of how such a transition in the distribution of responsibility is to be organized. In the Development Assistance Committee of the OECD we can already consult on common problems of economic aid. But there is more involved here than aid. We must find the machinery to concert within the Alliance at the highest level of responsibility our political policies toward these regions—a task that was impossible to conceive of when colonial disengagement dominated the scene but which becomes more realistic as our interest in these southern regions comes to rest on the problem of helping them maintain their independence, modernize their societies, and settle peacefully their differences with one another and with us to the north.

It is certain that in the years ahead one of the major tasks we confront is the improvement in our machinery of political consultation, not merely with respect to confrontations with the Communists but in carrying forward a more effective, constructive policy in the developing areas to the south.

A second great area of partnership lies, of course, in the field of nuclear weapons. The story begins, as we all know, with the Manhattan Project, in which the scientific talent of the West was organized in the United States to produce the first nuclear weapons. From this experience flowed the special nuclear relationship between the United States and Great Britain; and then there emerged the McMahon Act in which American policy sought to protect from the Communists the store of nuclear knowledge of which we were the major custodian.

As the 1950s proceeded, however, and the Soviet Union acquired thermonuclear weapons, the character of the problem, as seen from Washington, changed. The special nuclear relation to Great Britain was reinforced in 1958; and the need for security in certain nuclear matters remained—and remains—a real issue for the United States and the West, despite increasing Soviet virtuosity. But a new and great issue gradually came to the surface: How should nuclear affairs be organized within the Atlantic Alliance at a time when the resurgent wealth, confidence, and power of Western Europe no longer made a simple reliance on American nuclear power and the Anglo-American connection acceptable? The French *force de frappe,* initiated around 1956, represented an understandable impulse on the continent to play some meaningful role in shaping France's own destiny in a nuclear age, as well as an effort to achieve a nuclear status vis-à-vis the United States equivalent to that of Great Britain.

What are the solutions open to us? How can a community of sovereign nations, bound together by treaty, organize to maintain an effective nuclear deterrent in a period of cold war and for the use of nuclear weapons should their use be required in their common interest?

Theoretically one could conceive of a solution in which the European nations, having measured the full cost of national nuclear deterrents and the great advantages of a single, unified, unambiguous command over those weapons, should consciously forego the production of weapons and means of delivery and leave the job to the United States, while joining with us in intensive consultative arrangements for their operation and management. This is obviously a matter for the European nations to decide, for its raises fewer problems for the United States than any other solution. Moreover, no solution is conceivable that does not draw the European nations more deeply into the targeting, planning, and designing of strategy for nuclear weapons. But as we faced the facts, in the late 1950s and early 1960s, we were inclined to believe that this solution—of a mixed-manned committee working with the American nuclear force in an intimate consultative arrangement—was an insufficient answer. Great Britain and France were already launched on another path; and their science, technology, industry, and military establishments were increasingly caught up in nuclear affairs. Beyond that, it has been easy for us to understand why proud and free men, now fully recovered from the economic consequences of the second world war—men who have been threatened by Moscow over the past several years as hostages to the Soviet medium ballistic missiles lined up in Western Russia —would wish to play a larger, rather than a smaller, role in the deterrence of a nuclear attack. We understand why our friends in Europe may not be content, when threatened, merely to say to Moscow: Washington will protect us.

A second solution has been suggested by some on the European side of the Atlantic. They argue that the consequences of nuclear war are such, in the face of current and prospective Soviet capabilities, that one nation cannot rely on any other nation to come to its defense in the face of the danger of nuclear attack. Therefore, the only secure and dignified position for each nation is to command its own nuclear capability. Among our NATO allies a certain number have the industrial and technical capacity to produce nuclear weapons and some kind of delivery system. But if we were all to accept this theory, which denies the possibility of collective security arrangements in a nuclear age, two consequences would directly follow. First, the Alliance would fragment into a series of national nuclear capabilities, the European components of which would be inefficiently produced, unsystematically targeted, and quite unpersuasive in Moscow. Second, we would be proclaiming in the Alliance that no effective protection could be afforded to those among our allies who did not command a national nuclear capability. We would be inviting Moscow, in effect, to put diplomatic and military pressure on these smaller powers, one by one, in the face of a doctrine which asserted that no other nation would rationally protect them.

The acceptance of this doctrine could only mean the end of the North Atlantic Alliance—in fact the whole system of American alliances—opening the way for the fragmentation and piecemeal diplomatic or military defeat of Western Europe and other now free regions of the world.

In the light of these two marginal alternatives, it has been the policy of the American government, beginning with the latter days of the Eisenhower administration, to look toward arrangements which would increase the effective degree of partnership and participation in nuclear matters within the Atlantic Community, without diminishing the effectiveness and unity of our collective security deterrent. This is no simple matter in a world where fifteen nations are committed to a system of mutual defense but in which no unified sovereign institutions exist.

It has been natural for newspaper and other commentators to focus sharply on this ultimate problem: Whose finger will be on the trigger; whose finger, on the safety catch? Could the European forces fire their atomic weapons without the agreement of the United States? Could the United States fire without the agreement of Europe? Could individual nations within the Alliance veto firing by others? It has been our view that these ultimate questions could not and should not now be settled immediately and finally. The terms of the Atlantic partnership which evolve over coming months and years will depend on many factors, including, in particular, the way that the process of European unification, now temporarily frustrated, will proceed.

The nuclear matter within the Alliance is not only a question of Europe's relation to the United States but, at least equally, a question of the relative roll and status of European nations vis-à-vis one another. It may prove difficult to settle firmly the transatlantic nuclear relationship until the intra-European relationship takes clearer shape; and this problem is, evidently, linked to that of European unity.

It has been our view that four, more immediate courses of action should be considered urgently, which would move toward Atlantic partnership in nuclear matters. First, that we all commit ourselves to work toward a solution which would maintain the unity of the Alliance, with a unified nuclear deterrent at its core. Second, that we devise and agree on general guidelines for the use of nuclear weapons in the face of Soviet attack. Such agreed guidelines now exist for the defense of the NATO region. Third, that we take active steps to bring our European partners more deeply and directly into the nuclear business with respect to problems of targeting, control, and the strategic relationship between nuclear and conventional forces. Measures to this end are actively under way within NATO. Fourth, that we provide within this framework for active European (and Canadian) participation in the operation and control of strategic as well as tactical nuclear weapons. Out of the process of shared operational experience, consultation, and debate thus set in motion it has been our belief and our faith that a rational and sensible resolution of the control issue would emerge, acceptable to the peoples and parliaments of our allies and to our own people and the Congress. Moreover, we believe that this widened common experience may be essential for the development of a solidly agreed Atlantic military doctrine.

We would hope that the Inter-Allied Nuclear Force, now in an advanced stage of negotiation, will contribute to this end.

The major new instrument suggested by the United States to carry forward this process of intensified partnership is a mixed-manned multilateral nuclear force to be based at sea. This proposal, first made by Secretary Christian Herter at the NATO meeting of 1960, was reaffirmed by President Kennedy at Ottawa in May of 1961. In the autumn of 1962 an American technical mission, representing both the civil and military parts of our government, discussed how such a force might work with our NATO allies. As part of the Nassau agreement of December 1962, we stated that we would present this concept at a high political level to our allies. Acting as the President's personal representative, Ambassador Livingston Merchant began discussions at the North Atlantic Council itself and in a number of European capitals.

The fate of this proposal is in the hands of our European friends. We would hope that this path would come to commend itself not merely to the nonnuclear powers in NATO, but to those who now command or are building a national nuclear capability. We are convinced it is a technically viable way to widen the circle of participation in nuclear matters in a form which enhances the unity of the Alliance. It is also responsive to an important technical requirement of NATO: the need in the 1960s for an MRBM force to counter that now zeroed in on Western European targets from Russia. We are prepared to put into it our own men and money, and let its future evolve on the basis of shared experience and the evolution of thought and politics on both sides of the Atlantic.

As the most powerful member of the North Atlantic Alliance, bearing special responsibilities in the field of nuclear arms, we felt that we had a duty to lay before our friends a proposal which would permit an enlarged participation in nuclear matters within the Alliance in a form which would increase the unity of the Alliance rather than fragment it; and, in a tradition we share, we felt the way to begin was to begin and not debate and attempt to settle the now insoluble questions which are inherent in the sharing of nuclear responsibility in an alliance of multiple sovereignty.

Our discussions with our European friends have already had two important and useful effects. First, the European nations concerned have begun to come to grips with the real problems of the joint management of a nuclear deterrent. The discussions have been candid and mature. A matter which is bound to be the subject of heated and sometimes superficial debate is now being gripped in high seriousness by the NATO governments. Second, these discussions have suggested that there is an overwhelming commitment within the Alliance to move forward on a collective security basis. The dangers of fragmentation are now widely understood; and there is, in Ben Franklin's old phrase, a growing sense that in this decisive area we must hang together or we will hang separately.

The issues of political consultation and nuclear partnership do not, of course, exhaust the agenda of the Atlantic Alliance. We face major unsolved problems in the fields of trade, assistance to the underdeveloped areas, and the management of the free world's currencies and reserves. Building on the unsung but quite remarkable experience of intergovernmental cooperation, which has thus far helped keep us together in the face of Khrushchev's pressures on Berlin, we must learn better to concert our policies with respect to East-West relations. And down the line we shall have to think and work together in facing the implications for us all of the Chinese Communist effort to acquire nuclear weapons.

In all of these matters the instinct of American policy is to move forward pragmatically where we can, gathering experience and building up the most important asset an alliance can have: the confidence that comes and can only come from having solved real problems—even limited problems—together and successfully.

Undoubtedly, as progress is made old machinery will have to be modified and, perhaps, new machinery created. But the forums available to us now are ample, if the will to use them is effective.

All of us are, of course, wholly conscious of the difficulties we now face in the development of collective solutions within the Atlantic Alliance. The power of old-fashioned nationalism is, evidently, still considerable; and it is easy to understand how men, living in nations now miraculously revived and energetic, should hanker for a simpler world where nations form their policies on their own and concert them, where necessary, by the traditional means which diplomacy, as we have known it at an earlier time, could afford.

But the facts of the world in which we live and shall live do not permit us safely to indulge this nostalgia. We in the United States who are caught up in formal alliance with forty-two nations—and intimately bound to many more—know this perhaps better than most. Every move we make must take into account the implacable facts of interdependence. The nature of weapons, the immediacy of modern communications, the scope and the weight of the thrusts against us by the Communists, and, perhaps above all, the fact that virtually the whole of this planet is for the first time in history an intimate interacting political community, all make it clear that there is only one way for us to go if we are to preserve the values and interests of Western civilization; and that is toward the building of an Atlantic Community of which an increasingly united Europe is an integral part.

VI *The Role of Germany in the Evolution of World Politics*

If one looks at contemporary Germany and thinks back over the history of this century, it is clear that the internal condition of the Federal Republic of Germany and its role on the world scene represent an extraordinary achievement—certainly one of the greatest achievements of the postwar generation.

I am not referring here simply to the miracle of German economic recovery, in which a devastated nation, with an important part of its territory temporarily withdrawn, absorbed some 11 million refugees and then went on to rebuild itself and to create new levels of economic and social life for all its people.

I am thinking, rather, of the emergence of a stable, democratic government, rooted in a broad national consensus on foreign and domestic affairs transcending the major parties and freed of much of the bitterness and fragmentation which have marked democratic politics in parts of Europe in the past.

I am thinking of the steady loyalty of the Federal Republic of Germany to the concepts of both European integration and the Atlantic partnership. I am thinking of the expanding role of Germany as a constructive force in many parts of the world outside of Europe.

To understand the scale of this achievement one must look back at the history of modern Germany and the four major elements which converged to make that history difficult—difficult for Germany, for its neighbors, and for the world.

First, Germany was formed late among the modern nations. France, Britain, Russia, even the United States, had acquired a clear sense of national identity and nationhood when the German peoples were still struggling in the mid-nineteenth century to form an effective union. This accident of history tended to give Germany a sense that it had a lot to make up in a hurry before it could assume its rightful place in Europe and on the world scene. It made Germany at once less certain and more assertive in defining its national destiny.

Second, in its initial phase, German unity was dominated by the province of Prussia. That northeastern region had an old history of militarism, and it had been somewhat distant from the liberal currents of thought and feeling which ran through Western Europe, including Western Germany, in the late eighteenth century and, especially, during the French Revolution and its aftermath. There is a sense in which contemporary Germany represents the victory—and I believe the final victory—of the men who organized the liberal Frankfurt Parliament in 1848; although the revolution of 1848 was at the time captured by Prussia and the German nationalists.

Third, there is the simple fact of German energy, competence, and will to express its national feeling and identity in a large way on the world scene. In the context of European power politics between, say, 1860 and 1945, this thrust periodically created the greatest problems, since German ambitions clashed head-on with the vital interests of other nations, although there were substantial intervals when Germany found peaceful channels for the expression of its talent and national ambitions, enriching international life in many directions—for example, in science, education, literature, and every other dimension of Western cultural life.

Finally, there is the fact of geography: Germany is located astride the balance of power in Europe. It represents a critically important area, population, and concentration of resources between the East and the West. In the past, some Germans have been able to dream of using that position to dominate Europe. From the Communist point of view, in the pursuit of world power Germany remains the greatest possible prize.

Taken together, these elements of history, national gifts, and geography have been the cause of severe difficulty; but in the postwar years, the lessons of experience, painfully learned, have been given a constructive turn by the German people themselves, by their Western European neighbors, and, to a degree, by ourselves.

For we in the United States made important mistakes in our European policy between the two world wars and also had painful lessons to learn and to apply. By not joining the League of Nations and by not making our presence and military potential a steady factor in European security calculations, we helped create a situation which made it possible for Hitler to dream of German domination of Europe, and of European domination of the world. As I recall the diaries of Count Ciano, with their detailed account of the diplomacy of the Axis in the 1930s, there were virtually no references to the United States. Hitler and Mussolini dreamed their dreams and made their plans as if the United States did not exist as a factor in Europe's power balance. Our isolationism between the wars helped encourage this tragic parochialism.

Reading this lesson in the immediate postwar days, the American government sought to make a policy toward the European continent which would avoid the mistakes of earlier times.

It was on this view of the problem of Europe and Germany that we built the Marshall Plan. We played our part in constructing NATO; we backed the Coal and Steel Community and EURATOM; and we supported the Common Market. It is within this policy, to which German leadership creatively responded, that the Federal Republic of Germany has found its way back to a role of dignity, equality, and leadership within Western Europe itself, in the councils of the Atlantic Community, and on the world scene.

I believe the German people and their political leaders understand better than most that the real problems they confront and we in the West confront can only be solved by integrated European action and Atlantic partnership.

In terms of history, they have—with authentic insight and sincerity—put aside the old rivalry with France and made the Franco-German *rapprochement* a major long-term object of policy, to be achieved within the framework of an integrated European Community and sound Atlantic partnership.

In military affairs the Germans live, after all, on an exposed frontier of the free world. They understand that the protection of that frontier and of West Berlin has been achieved over the years not by gestures or by self-imposed Communist restraint, but by a massive mobilization of military resources and an evident will to use them. They understand that the military strength of the United States—in underground silos, in Polaris submarines under the seas, on aircraft carriers, alert on airbases all over the world, standing in ready reserve in the United States—is a critical and irreplaceable component of their security, along with the United States garrison in Berlin and United States troops side by side with their own on German soil, and with all the other contingents and commitments that NATO represents.

With their economic life interwoven intimately with that of every part of Europe, they understand that their prosperity hinges on an outward-looking policy of trade—with policies that widen rather than narrow the areas embraced within a low-tariff trading system. They have supported the concept of genuine economic integration in Europe—common organs with substantial powers of decision—and have been willing to make substantial sacrifices to make it work.

They have, moreover, seen economic integration as a way station to other forms of European unity, involving political as well as economic relations among the other European states.

Shorn of colonies by history, and freed in this generation from the responsibilities and burdens of helping manage the great transition from colonialism, Germany has been able to approach the problems of the underdeveloped countries on a world-wide basis and with a fresh vision of the task and its opportunities.

With some quarter of a million American troops located in Germany for the defense of an essentially common frontier, the German government has understood the strain on our balance of payments imposed by our commitment to the collective defense of the free world and has been sympathetic and helpful in cushioning some of its consequences.

Finally, looking to the east and to those 18 million Germans still held against their will within an essentially occupation regime, but understanding also the nature of the nuclear age, the Germans have pursued the struggle for self-determination and for national unity by peaceful means and as part of the Western coalition.

In short, reading the lessons of their experience and the common experience of this century, looking soberly at their problems as a nation, studying modern military technology and the nature of modern communications, the Germans have understood that none of us in the West—including, of course, the United States—can solve our problems unless we make common cause, unless we build policies on a common loyalty to Western values and the great Western tradition of which we are all a part. They have understood that the task with which we have been confronted since 1945 and which still confronts us, includes, but transcends, older concepts of nationalism, national defense, and national destiny.

We have every reason to believe that the cast of German

policy is firmly set in all the major political parties and in the minds and hearts of the German people—including the younger generation now emerging, which never really knew the days of Hitler. But the modern world is so intimately interwoven that we in the United States bear a part of the responsibility for maintaining the continuity of German policy.

First, we must remain not merely a reliable ally to Germany but a true partner with Germany in helping maintain within NATO the defense of the Western frontier, including West Berlin. The German contribution to its own and to Western defense has expanded and matured. We are both engaged, with some of our NATO allies, in exploring the setting up within NATO of a multilateral nuclear force, which would offer European nations self-respecting participation in nuclear deterrence without leading to national nuclear proliferation. We are both engaged with all our NATO allies in refining our strategic doctrine, in moving toward an agreed NATO defense policy for the nuclear age, and in designing the courses which would make that doctrine steadily effective.

The stability of German policy hinges on the continued success of the collective defense of Western Europe and on Germany's role as a respected senior partner in that effort.

We have demonstrated in the past two years in the Berlin and Cuban crises that the commitment of the United States to collective defense has survived the Soviet acquisition of nuclear weapons and the Soviet ability to damage the United States grievously in a nuclear war. The Soviet tactics of nuclear blackmail, mounted in 1958 against Berlin and pursued down to 1962, failed. The first condition for the stability of the West is that such tactics continue to fail, should they be again attempted.

Second, in a period when we are seeking to reduce the dangers and tensions of the cold war and to establish how far we can move safely toward the control of armaments, it is essential that we consult in greatest intimacy with our allies where their interests may be involved. It is for that reason that we resisted in Moscow all pressures to link the nuclear test ban to a non-aggression pact between NATO and the Warsaw powers. The Atlantic partnership is more than a defensive alliance. It is a group of nations with a common heritage and large abiding common interests. We are evidently prepared to fight together. But we must learn to work with equal intimacy in exploring the opportunities for moving gradually toward a more peaceful world.

We consulted almost daily, in the greatest operational detail, in dealing with the Berlin crisis of 1961–1962. We intend to consult with equal intimacy in exploring the possibilities which may open up in the months ahead for easing the dangers and tensions of the cold war. And in these consultations the issue of Germany still split, its people still denied the rights of self-determination, must be dealt with by Germany and Germany's allies with the greatest concern and seriousness.

Third, we must support Germany, within whatever degree of unity Europe comes to achieve, to play a maximum role in all the great creative enterprises of the free world, already extensive but still expanding: In the adventure of aid to the underdeveloped countries; in designing policies of trade, not merely within Europe and as between Europe and the United States, but on a world basis, where all of us must find ways of creating a trade framework beneficial at once to the more developed and less developed nations of the free world community; and in monetary affairs, where we must fashion in the 1960s new ways of underpinning a flow of trade and capital movements which is increasing much faster than the world's gold supply.

Although our bilateral relations with Germany are intimate and intensive—and they should be, since together we bear a very high proportion of the burden of European defense—we are ultimately bound together by loyalty to a larger vision. The vision has three parts: the unity of Europe, the building of the Atlantic Community, and the systematic deployment of the energies and the resources of the Atlantic Community for the larger purposes of world peace and prosperity.

This vision is evidently still incomplete: European unity is in an interval of pause and debate—by no means the first such interval since 1945. Involved in this debate is, of course, Britain's long-run relationship to the European continent. Partly because the European debate also concerns the appropriate long-run relation between the United States and a united Europe, certain issues in the transatlantic partnership remain stalled, although there is more quiet progress forward than the newspapers record.

It should neither surprise nor dismay us that movement toward these goals—supported equally by all four of our postwar presidents—should be slow. This is the biggest piece of international architecture ever undertaken at a time of peace by sovereign nations. Great issues are at stake in each country, reaching deep into both their history and their current politics.

But as President Kennedy made clear on his trip to Europe in June 1963, we remain firmly committed to support the highest degree of European unity Europeans themselves can organize, within the larger framework of an Atlantic partnership.

We remain loyal to this vision—now embedded in United States policy for almost a generation—not because of inertia and not without understanding the difficulties inherent in its pursuit. We remain committed to it because it best serves the interests of the United States, the interests of Europe, and the interests of freedom everywhere.

Although this policy took shape in response to Stalin's immediate postwar effort to take over an impoverished and disheartened Western Europe, it is not dependent, in our judgment, on the persistence of active Soviet thrusts against the

West of the kind we have seen, for example, over Berlin in the period 1958–1962. We need a unified Europe working in partnership across the Atlantic for reasons that go deeper into the times in which we live and the problems we shall face.

The nature of military technology—and Communist nuclear capabilities—decrees that the Atlantic Community is about the smallest unit which can organize a rational and effective defense of Europe. The problem of organizing a community of independent nations embracing both the advanced nations of the northern part of the free world and the rapidly emerging nations of Asia, the Middle East, Africa, and Latin America equally requires that we work in concert across the Atlantic. The problems posed for us by negotiations with Moscow, looking toward control of atomic weapons, touch vital interests of each nation of the Atlantic Community, which require resolution within the family; and so, ultimately, does the problem of Communist China, its present aggressive disposition, and its future, notably when Communist China acquires a nuclear capability.

Peering ahead with all the imagination of which we are capable we cannot conceive of a time relevant to current planning in which it would not be to the advantage of Europe to unite and to work in concert with North America.

Put another way, we can see nothing but danger to us all if Europe should separate itself from the United States or if it should regard its great prosperity and the recent easing of tensions with Moscow as an occasion in which old-fashioned nationalism can again be given free rein.

Communist authorities have said two things which are worth noting about the recent period of relaxed tension. First, there shall be no ideological coexistence. This means that they conceive of the present negotiations as limited to one phase—one important phase—of the cold war: namely, efforts to reduce the danger that a nuclear war might come about which would be neither to their interests nor to ours. It means also that the Communists intend to persist, with every other means at their disposal, in pressing for the expansion of Communist power and influence. All the information at the command of the government, watching the behavior of Communists in every quarter of the globe, suggests that they have in no way reduced their efforts to expand their power and influence at the expense of the West.

The second thing they have said is that they hope and expect in a period of slackened tension that what they call the "inherent contradictions" of the West will increasingly assert themselves. They hope and expect that, with the crises in Berlin and elsewhere somewhat less acute, that we in the West will not have the wit to stick together; and they evidently intend to exploit any schisms among us that might open up.

These are warnings we should take seriously; and they relate to the maintenance within Germany of the kind of politics and policy which, as I said earlier, represent one of the greatest collective achievements of the postwar period.

I am confident that Germans and German policy will remain loyal to the concepts of European unity and the Atlantic partnership and to the collective defense of the values of Western civilization which underlie that policy.

The issues on our common agenda in the West have changed in recent months, as indeed they have often changed over the period since about 1947 when the present policy was launched. The policies of the Atlantic nations have exhibited in these two decades a great resilience. We have survived problems and crises of many kinds, leaving the bone structure of NATO still intact and the impulse toward European unity still vital. We have dealt with problems of economic reconstruction in Europe and foreign aid in the developing nations; with a wide range of issues in trade and monetary affairs. We have dealt with thrusts against Turkey and Greece and twice with major thrusts against Berlin. We have adjusted our common strategy from a time when the major threat was the Red Army on the ground to the increasing complexity of an era when the Soviet Union commanded a nuclear arsenal and the means to deliver it with missiles. We are in the process of moving from a time of United States nuclear monopoly to one where the burdens and responsibilities of nuclear defense are increasingly shared. We have seen moments close to war and have had substantial intervals of relatively relaxed tension between Moscow and the West. We have seen relations between the West and Eastern Europe move from the black despair of Stalin's time to a period where men on both sides of the Iron Curtain can look forward with greater hope to increasing degrees of national independence and human freedom in the East and to rebuilding old lines of connection that derive from the common religions and cultural basis of Eastern and Western Europe. We have seen Western Europe survive a series of difficult crises in the old colonial areas and move toward new relations of association and partnership with the former colonies and with other nations now emerging into the world under the banners of national independence and modernization.

All of these adjustments have not gone easily; and being democratic societies, the difficulties have been there for all to see. Our debates are out in the open. But we have every reason for faith that the policies, machinery, and attitudes of mind built up in the postwar generation will evolve in ways which will enhance the unity of the West—not fragment it.

To this end Germany has now a great role to play. No nation has a greater stake in the success of a collective policy in the West or more capacity to give it substance. Germany's postwar security, prosperity, domestic tranquility, and growing stature on the world scene are rooted in that policy; and what Germans and Germany have already achieved now makes it possible for them actively to lead in carrying it forward into the next phase of Western history. But so interconnected is the world in which we live that the steadfastness of all, in particular, that of us in the United States—still the inescapable leaders of the West—must remain unaltered.

If we retain as a nation our loyalty to the large objectives of European unity and the Atlantic partnership we can feel confident not merely of the stability of German policy but of the steady progress of the cause of freedom in every quarter of the globe.

Part III

North-South Problems

VII Strategy and Economics

The nations of Asia, the Middle East, Africa, and Latin America are in the midst of the process of modernizing their societies. Some are well along that road; others are just beginning. What we sometimes call underdeveloped nations represent a very wide spectrum, with different problems marking each stage along the road to self-sustained growth. And in the end, each nation, like each individual, is in an important sense unique. What is common throughout these regions is that men and women are determined to bring to bear what modern science and technology can afford in order to elevate the standards of life of their peoples and to provide a firm basis for positions of national dignity and independence on the world scene.

The United States is firmly committed as a nation to support this effort. We look forward to the emergence of strong assertive nations which, out of their own traditions and aspirations, create their own forms of modern society. We take it as our duty to help maintain the integrity and the independence of the modernization process going forward in many parts of the world—insofar as our resources and our ability to influence the course of events permit.

That possibility is challenged by Communist objectives and Communist policy. The Communists also perceive that the process of modernization involves fundamental social, political, and economic change. These are bound to be turbulent times; and it is the Communist intent to exploit the turbulence of this transitional process in order to seize power and to mold the emerging world in their image and link it tightly to the Communist empire.

It is often said that what we can observe in the contemporary world is a struggle between two blocs. This is not the case. What is at stake is whether a new world order shall be created by the voluntary association and cooperation of independent nations—each having fashioned its own modern personality—or a world order, dominated from a single center, of nations forced into a single mold.

We in the United States can live comfortably in a pluralistic world, because our life at home is based on the principle of cooperation among dignified equals; but the Communists are driven, by their methods for organizing power, to violate equally the integrity of individuals and of nations. Thus, when seeking power, they aim to associate themselves with all manner of forward-looking human and national aspirations. Once in power, they drag from the shelves their dreary archaic handbooks and impose a pattern of organization which runs against the grain of human and national character and personality. In the end, that is why the Communist offensive will fail.

We have not forgotten the lesson of Korea. We cannot assume the Communists will not again overtly cross frontiers with military force; and our dispositions with respect to the SEATO and CENTO areas and elsewhere take that possibility into account; but it is also clear that for some years they have been relying heavily on the possibility of exploiting the internal turbulence which inevitably comes with the drive toward modernization to seize power from within.

In defense of the independence of nations and the national integrity of the modernization process, we are, therefore, equally concerned with problems of defense and with the constructive tasks of development.

I have for many years been professionally interested in the problems of economic development; and there are those who may find it odd for an economist to be also concerned—as I have been—with the problems of countering Communist methods of guerrilla warfare and subversion. But it is, in fact, quite natural for a student of modernization to interest himself in the economic, social, and political development of Vietnam and also in its protection against indirect invasion from the north; with the Alliance for Progress and also the defense of Latin America from the infection which the Communists are seeking to impose upon it; and with all the related military and constructive activities elsewhere in the developing areas. For Communism is not the wave of the future—it is a disease of the transitional process which well-trained, well-organized professional cadres seek to impose on societies at the early stages of modernization.

In any case the policy of my government is to do what it can both to assist those who would modernize their societies and to help them defend their national independence as modernization goes forward. We must build together, and we must protect what we are building.

As we move into the 1960s all of us in the free world are trying to consolidate and to build on the lessons we have learned about economic development since the end of the second world war.

The first lesson is that aid from outside a country can only be helpful to its development to the extent that the government and people of a nation organize their own resources. Economic growth is primarily a national enterprise. Development cannot and should not be wholly viewed in national terms; and, certainly, external assistance is important; but the heart of economic development consists in national measures of self-help.

Second, national planning of the development process is required as a basis both for the domestic mobilization of resources and effective foreign aid. National plans are needed because, as Adam Smith noted long ago—when prescribing for underdeveloped Britain of the eighteenth century—governments must create the framework within which a modern economy can develop. It is the government which must organize and finance the educationl system and shape it to the nation's needs. It is the government which must lay out and, in most cases, finance the fundamental social overhead projects—in transport, electric power, and other sectors—on which development depends. It is the government which must solve problems of land tenure and create the framework within which agricultural productivity can be improved by the individual peasant. It is the government which must assure that the savings of the community are effectively mobilized by equitable taxation, so that investment projects can be financed without inflation and on terms the people will regard as fair. It is the government which must devise policies which insure that the foreign accounts are kept in balance and that the development effort is not frustrated by a foreign exchange crisis.

These minimal functions were performed by governments even in nations most deeply committed to private enterprise, blessed with ample land and an old tradition of private entrepreneurship—like Canada and the United States. In our own time, and where these initial circumstances do not exist, governments may have to go further and help set the national targets for the private enterprise sector, or even, for a time, manage a portion of the industrial system.

It may seem strange that we in the United States, who are so deeply attached to the virtues of private enterprise, should be the advocates of national planning in the underdeveloped areas. There is, in fact, no incompatibility between a belief that national planning is essential in the early stages of development and a belief in the wisdom of leaving to private enterprise a wide and expanding range of economic activities. How wide that range is each country will, of course, decide for itself in the light of its own problems and possibilities. But the framework within which a modern private enterprise system can develop must, in large part, be created initially by the effort and initiative of governments. It is this perception which has drained away much of the fervor from the argument about government versus private enterprise in the development process—an argument which, even a few years ago, seemed to be central to the whole business. As nations have acquired practical experience in economic development, it is becoming increasingly clear that each of the two sectors has a job to do and that their jobs are supplementary and mutually reinforcing.

When self-sustained and regular growth has been attained—and even in the process of attaining that stage—the natural course of events is for the private sector to expand rapidly. The development of private enterprise over the past decade in India and Pakistan is, for example, illuminating. The most immediate reason for this evolution is that efficiency in producing many diverse products is hard for a government bureaucracy to attain. Besides, there are not that many competent bureaucratic managers.

The lesson of history is that the interests of an advancing society are best served when the bulk of industry and agriculture is managed by individuals or firms forced by competition to maximum efficiency, their accounts reflecting true costs, and their output responsive to the changing tastes of the people. We have learned, both in the less developed and more developed nations, when such competitive private sectors have emerged, that their emergence in no way need divert resources away from the objectives laid down in a national plan. In India, for example, the vitality of the private enterprise sector and the direction of its development are essential ingredients in current national planning.

In the United States, Western Europe, and Japan we have found that there are ample indirect means for insuring that a massive private enterprise sector can keep within the bounds of the common interest and, in fact, be an essential reinforcement to it.

Although national planning is crucial to the development

process—notably when nations are approaching the stage of take-off into self-sustained growth—we have also come to understand what is involved in making a plan effective. Good paper plans are not enough. With all due respect to my profession, economists cannot build roads, or administer power plants, or go out to the villages to teach more efficient ways of growing food.

An effective plan must be backed by the whole administrative apparatus of the state—not merely its planning organization. It must be capable of generating feasibility studies and blueprints for individual projects. It must provide not only goals but the means to achieve those goals step by step, day by day. And, in the end, the plan must engage the minds and hearts of the people—from the cabinet to the villages.

A third lesson of our postwar experience is that foreign aid is likely to be most effective if it is geared into national development programs on a long-term basis. In committing themselves and their peoples to ambitious development goals—and demanding the sacrifices and efforts which are necessary for their fulfillment—it is natural that governments should wish to know in advance how much foreign aid they can count on over any planning period.

American foreign aid legislation has now taken this factor into account; and we have been joined by our partners in Western Europe, Canada, and Japan. We are rapidly learning to weave together the national and international contributions to development in a systematic way, and we look forward to extending this method as new national development programs come forward. We would expect the OECD and its Development Assistance Committee to become an increasingly important instrument for this collaborative purpose, as time goes on.

A fourth lesson is this: Although we are still learning this job together—and have much to learn—we are confident that the methods of free men will prove more effective than the apparently more efficient techniques of totalitarian regimes.

It is true that a powerful police system, combined with a disciplined single party, can get many things done—especially things which relate directly to the maintenance and the extension of the system's power; but as we watch the evolution of the developing nations run by Communist governments, and as we look back on the lessons of our own experience, there is increasing reason to believe that systems of society committed to the maintenance of individual freedom—and its essential counterpart, individual responsibility—have proved more efficient as well as more humane than those which seek by forced draft and the power of the state to drive development forward by totalitarian methods.

Only a few years back, it was common to believe that, whatever their demerits, Communist societies had the capacity to sustain much higher rates of growth than societies based on human freedom. This is a proposition which can no longer be scientifically maintained. Leaving aside Communist China, which has gone through a radical decline in its economic fortunes, here are some current growth rate figures for recent years: In 1962 the rate of growth in the gross national product for the nations under Communist governments was 3.6 per cent. For the NATO nations the figure was 4.8 per cent. The figure for the Soviet Union itself was somewhat under 4 per cent; for the United States, recovering from recession, a higher than average 5.4 per cent.

These data may vary over the years. But the fact is that the economic gap between the free world and the Communist bloc widened; and the same is true, of course, in the grand historical competition between the development of Communist China and the two great nations of the Indian subcontinent, which, against great difficulties, continue to make regular progress with societies rooted in the principle of consent.

I cite these figures not because rates of growth are the decisive measure of a society's worth. Our values begin with the integrity of the individual and his equality under God and the law. They extend to the right of nations to shape their lives in the light of their own history, culture, and aspirations, protected by the principle of self-determination.

Quite aside from the inhumanity of Communist methods, it appears to be a technical fact that the most powerful system of control is an inadequate substitute for the incentives and commitment of the individual citizen, once he can be engaged. Development is a process which requires that millions of human beings and many organized groups assume responsibility for moving things forward on their narrow part of the front. There are simply not enough Communist cadres or secret policemen available to substitute for the energy and commitment of men and women who understand what needs to be done and why it is in their interest to do it.

This weakness of communism is most apparent in the field of agriculture. Communist methods have managed to shift one Communist country after another from food surplus to food deficit status; and the Soviet Union itself must maintain perhaps twice the working force in agriculture it would need if its leaders were not committed to the method of control they feel necessary for the political safety of the regime.

This is no trivial matter; for an increase in agricultural productivity is required not merely to feed the people and the expanding cities: It is essential for the development of industry and industrial markets and for the maintenance of a healthy balance-of-payments situation. The vast general economic crisis in Communist China should be studied as a lesson in the crucial importance of agricultural productivity to the development process as a whole.

The difference between Communist planning and planning in the free world comes to this: Communist planning is a device for maximum political control over the individual—and it thereby burdens the state with functions it cannot efficiently carry and destroys individual incentives needed for a vital economy; planning for underdeveloped countries in the free world is a device for assuring balance in the growth process and for creating a framework within which individual incentives and individual initiative can be effective.

In short, the lesson of our experience thus far is that we should be confident that in going forward with economic development by the methods of pragmatic planning and individual consent which are natural to us, we are on the right track technically as well as morally.

We have drawn, then, from the first phase of postwar experience with development an awareness that foreign aid can only be helpful in proportion to the efforts of self-help within a country; an understanding of the crucial role of national development plans in creating the framework for the whole development process; an understanding of the need to make available foreign aid on a long-term basis in relation to national development plans; and an inner confidence that while the tasks ahead are enormous, there is no reason to believe that communism represents a technique of organizing for development which cannot be outmatched by the methods of more open societies if we put our minds fully to the task.

VIII *The Challenge of Democracy in Developing Nations*

There is no more important subject, for both social science and policy, than the relation between economic and political development, and there is no subject about which we all have more to learn.

We have made considerable progress in ordering our thoughts on the requirements for regular economic growth, but what about the requirements for stable democracy? Why is it so difficult to maintain stable democratic practices in societies caught up in the transition from traditional to modern forms of economic and social organization? Is movement towards stable democracy a general and natural trend?

II

It may be helpful to begin with a broad answer to this question: What, in general, are the tasks of government?

Whether one considers an ancient Chinese dynasty or an advanced society in the contemporary world, governments must exercise power in three major directions:

1. To protect the society's territorial integrity; or, more generally, to secure or advance the nation's interests in the international arena of power, as those interests are defined by those who wield effective power.

2. To provide for the general welfare, as welfare and the government's responsibility for welfare are generally defined within the society.

3. To preserve the constitutional order; that is, to maintain public order, orderly change, and legitimate succession by some enforceable balance between public constraint and individual freedom of action and expression of opinion.

The tasks of national security, the norms of welfare, the character and solidity of the constitutional order, and the balances struck between the maintenance of public order and the freedom of the citizenry have varied over the centuries in particular societies and as among societies in particular periods.

But the heart of politics and of political debate lies in these three fundamental questions, from ancient times down to the election issues of 1964, from simple tribes to elaborate industrial societies, from advanced democracies to totalitarian dictatorships.

III

If these are the eternal tasks of government, how shall we define democracy?

Democracy represents one way of solving the third of the basic tasks of government—reconciling public order with consent—and of shaping policy with respect to the other two tasks: the security and welfare of the society.

Democracy proceeds from the judgment that the policies of governments should flow from the regular and active expression of judgment and choice by all of a nation's citizens who wish to express their views. Democracy recognizes, in the political process as elsewhere, that the talents, tastes, and interests of citizens are not identical: the provision of equality of opportunity is the critical objective. Thus, even in a vigorous democracy the expression of consent goes forward by a process of representation which places important power and responsibilities in the hands of those who effectively lead the major groups in a society.

Virtually all systems of government claim the consent of the governed, but many count on raising the cost of dissent to such a high level, by repression or other sanctions, that consent consists merely in submission—the absence of open revolt or of massive public disorder. Democracy lowers the cost of dissent to the minimum and creates lawful procedures for the active and explicit registering of consent, so that opposition will always exist and rightly know that its ideas and interests can be given effect, if they achieve majority status.

Democracy is, thus, a method of government which forces government to seek and then to reflect the active will—rather than the passive consent—of the governed.

Behind this priority lie four value judgments which determine the direction toward which those who believe in democracy seek to move.

1. Individual human beings represent a unique balancing of impulses and aspirations which, despite the conscious and unconcious external means that help shape them, are to be accorded a moral and even religious respect. The underlying aim of society is to permit these individual complexes of impulses and aspirations to have their maximum expression, compatible with the well-being of other individuals and the security of society.

2. Governments thus exist to assist individuals to achieve their own fulfillment in ways consonant with the need to protect individual human beings from the harm they might do one another and to protect organized societies against the aggression of other societies.

3. Governments can take their shape legitimately only from some effective expression of the combined will and judgments of individuals: on the basis of one man one vote.

4. Some men aspire to power over their fellow men and derive satisfaction from the exercise of power aside from the purposes to which power is put. This fundamental human quality in itself makes dangerous to the well-being of society the concentration of political power in the hands of individuals and groups even where these groups may constitute a majority. Reliable con-

stitutional and legal measures to protect the position of the minority are, therefore, fundamental to the democratic concept.

From Plato on, political scientists have recognized that men may not understand their own best interests, and, in particular, that they may be passive, shortsighted, or swayed by urgent emotions in their definition of that interest. As between the individual's limitation in defining wisely his own long-run interest and his inability to exercise power wisely over others, without check, democratic societies have broadly chosen to risk the former rather than the latter danger in the organization of society, and to diminish the former danger by popular education, by the inculcation of habits of individual responsibility, and by devices of government which temper the less thoughtful political reactions of men. From Plato to contemporary Communist totalitarianism, however, there have been those who have chosen, intellectually, in practice, or both, to risk the latter danger.

From this definition, the democratic element within a society emerges as a matter of degree, of aspiration, and direction of movement. The pure democratic conception is compromised to some extent in all organized societies. It is compromised by the inescapable process of representation, by the need to protect individuals from each other, by the need to protect the society as a whole from others, and by the checks installed to protect the workings of the society from man's frequent inability to define wisely his own long-run interest. Even when societies strive for the democratic compromise, the balance between liberty and order which any society can achieve and still operate effectively, and the particular form that balance will take, are certain to vary. This balance and the form it takes will vary not only from society to society, but also at various periods within one society —in response to that society's history and cultural heritage, the state of education of its citizens, and the nature of the problems it confronts as a domestic community and on the world scene.

Aware of the abiding weakness of man as a social animal, the democrat leans, nevertheless, to the doctrine of "trust the people" rather than "Father knows best." And he gives substance to that inclination by lowering the cost of dissent to the minimum compatible with public order and the security of the state and by supporting regular competitive elections to determine who shall control the levers of power and what the cast of national policy shall be.

IV

The successful working of democracy requires certain preconditions. Three essential and interrelated preconditions appear to be these.

First, there must be a relatively broad consensus within the society on the main directions of both foreign and welfare policy; that is, on the substance of the first two basic tasks of government. In the United States, for example, public opinion polls suggest that on most great issues there has been a bipartisan majority of something like 60 per cent in support of major new policies adopted; something like 25 per cent remains normally opposed; and perhaps 15 per cent remains without conviction, even after an issue has been widely aired in public. To establish a consensus that broad on a major issue in turn demands both determined advocacy and public education by the political leadership and a willingness to compromise—a process carried forward in the United States within the two major parties, as well as between them, and between the Executive and the Congress. The ability of a society, through its representative leaders, to find effective consensus on the great issues, while permitting factional competition and compromise to settle lesser issues, is perhaps the most fundamental condition for stable democracy.

The second condition is a sense within the minority that their basic rights will be protected as well as their ability to continue to express freely and effectively their dissident views as part of a living political process. The classic formulation of these universally protected rights was Jefferson's life, liberty, and the pursuit of happiness. And it is a central function of the judicial system to assure that life is not taken, liberty infringed, or the pursuit of private satisfaction frustrated without due process of law.

Third, the whole political process must be underpinned by a widespread loyalty to democratic values and to the continuity of the democratic process itself, notably among those who lead the society's major groups. Individual citizens and substantial groups in the society must be prepared, from time to time, to accept some short-run damage to their interests on behalf of a larger communal interest in maintaining a stable competitive political system. There must be, in short, an important element of loyalty to the constitutional arrangements transcending special interests.

Modern history suggests that the maintenance of even well-grounded democratic political systems is not automatic. It is an endless task, even for societies that have a long experience of democratic practice; and success is not guaranteed.

The American Civil War, for example, resulted from a sense within an important minority of the population that what it regarded as its basic and essential rights would not be protected if it remained within the Union, as the United States—and its electoral system—expanded to embrace the whole sweep of territory out to the Pacific.

In 1933 German democracy broke down, primarily because of an extremely deep and protracted depression: a failure of the state to meet what were widely judged to be minimum welfare requirements.

The continuity of postwar French democracy was broken in 1958, due to the inability of the French political process to deal with the Algerian problem.

The factors bearing on these three illustrative cases are, of course, more complex than I suggest here, but they demonstrate a valid proposition: Breakdowns in the continuity of democracy have come about when consensus was broken on a great issue—when some purposeful minority within a population revolted in response to what it believed to be a gross failure under one or more of the three basic categories of national policy: policy toward national security; domestic welfare; or the workings of the political process itself, under existing constitutional arrangements.

It is evident, then, that high levels of income and of literacy, a command over advanced technology, a well-established sense of nationhood, and even a substantial prior history of democratic political experience do not, in themselves, guarantee the continuous and successful workings of the political democracy. Nevertheless, there does appear to be some relationship between the degree of modernization of a society, in the broadest sense, and its tendency to generate a relatively competitive democratic political system.

In 1960, at the Center for International Studies at M.I.T., indexes of modernization were worked out for developing areas in Asia, the Middle East, Africa, and Latin America. These indexes were then compared with a rough estimate of the degree of competition in the political system of some sixty contemporary nation-states—the degree of competition being taken as a shorthand way of measuring the democratic element in the political process. The indexes of modernization reflected not merely income per head in the society, but the degree of education, the availability of medical services, the proportion of the population in urban areas, the intensity of communications, and the degree of industrialization. When these indexes were set off against a rough ordering of the degree of democracy in their respective political systems, there was, as one would expect, a broad tendency of the more modern of the developing countries to create and sustain a more highly competitive political structure; but the exceptions were highly significant.

India, for example, ranked high in terms of the degree of democracy it has thus far proved capable of sustaining, but its level of income per capita and other indexes of modernization are relatively low. It is evident in this and some other cases that factors beyond the degree of modernization are at work: for example, the extent to which its political and other public leaders are committed to democratic practice; the extent to which a modern legal system has been created and widely accepted; the quality of the civil service; and, above all, whether some broad working consensus on the major goals of foreign and domestic policy has been developed among those who wield or seek to wield influence on public affairs.

At the other end of the spectrum there were cases where a relatively high degree of modernization was associated with a low democratic rating. Cuba, for example, was such a case. By the late 1950's Cuba had developed a high degree of modernization, as measured in conventional indexes, but—under both Batista and Castro—Cuba failed to develop the substantive consensus and the other basic conditions necessary for the working of a stable political democracy.

As a first approximation, then, one can assert these three propositions:

First, modernization of a society in its technical dimensions appears to be an important factor in creating the conditions for the management of a stable modern democratic political system, but modernization is not a sufficient or determining condition. We still have much to learn about the precise interconnections between modernization and political democracy.

Second, successful democracy requires a high degree of consensus on the substance of policy, an assured degree of protection for the minority, and a widespread loyalty to the constitutional system itself.

Third, a gross failure in any of the three substantive tasks of government—security, welfare, or the Constitution itself—can jeopardize the continuity of even a well-grounded democratic system.

V

Against this background it is possible to describe why the early stages of economic modernization and development often give rise to political turbulence.

The bringing into a mainly traditional and agricultural society of modern technology alters the view within that society of each of the three major tasks of government.

First, development is likely to produce a new view of the developing nation's appropriate international status. The impulse to modernization often derives, in part, from the desire of a nation's effective leaders to develop greater stature and dignity for that nation on the world scene. Nations have often shaken themselves out of the traditional patterns and accepted the burdens and opportunities of modernization in response to the intrusion of more advanced societies—whether that intrusion was military, political, or economic. This nationalist reaction has not been, of course, the only motivation which has led men to begin the tasks of economic development; they have been moved also, for example, by a desire to lengthen and enrich the lives of their children and to provide higher levels of welfare for their citizens. But a redefinition of a nation's role on the world scene has usually accompanied the modernization process. And the requirements of modernization—in trade, capital, and the acquisition of new technology—bring about, in themselves, new international relationships.

Second, modernization brings with it new hopes and expectations about the level of welfare men can expect, and it simultaneously lays upon governments new specific tasks which are essential in establishing the preconditions for sustained industrial growth, notably in education, public works, and agriculture. The execution of these tasks in turn requires that the state learn how to collect (and that the society accept the collection of) enlarged resources through taxation. In short, modernization changes both the role of government and the citizen's expectations of what the government should provide by way of public welfare.

Third, modernization tends to shift the balance of power and influence in the society away from rural areas—away from those who own land—to the cities, into the hands of those who can manipulate and administer the instruments of modernization. Whether accompanied by formal changes in constitutional arrangements or not, modernization alters the structural characteristics of political life.

Since modernization is a process which takes place over a substantial period of time, it follows that developing societies face certain inherent conflicts between the old patterns of life and public policy and emerging new patterns. One must expect within such societies some difficulty in achieving an effective consensus on the substance of both foreign and domestic policy. One must expect a measure of disappointment at the pace at which new expectations of increased welfare are fulfilled. One must expect that the machinery of government will only gradually acquire skill and efficiency in their modern functions. One must expect that there will be resistance among those who have the most to lose or least to gain from the transition from a predominantly agricultural to an urban, commercial, and industrial society—as well as resistance from those who find change itself painful.

One must even expect that the conflict will be internal; that is, men and women will be torn within themselves by the attractions and imperatives of modernization on the one hand, and by the habits and commitments to older ways of looking at things on the other.

These inherent characteristics of the transitional process—rendering difficult the achievement of the underlying requirements for democracy—make the successful operation of political democracy such a challenging task in the early stages of economic development—what I have called the preconditions period.

But as the society moves out of the preconditions into take-off —where sustained forward momentum becomes evident and regular—these difficulties may begin to ease. The very fact of progress, even over a limited front, evokes the vision of a common future in which the fruits of modernization will be widely shared. The leaders in the modernization process—in government, industry, commerce, and the working force—develop the attitudes as well as the skills necessary to carry forward the absorption of modern science and technology, including the skills of modern government and business administration. With enlarging income and tax collection, it is possible to widen the range of those who share the benefits of modernization, through health, education, and other welfare measures. Meanwhile, more active experience on the world scene begins to establish the possibilities and limits for the nation's enlarged international role.

In short, a successful take-off begins to bring about some of the conditions which make possible the emergence of stable democratic practice. Above all, modernization itself becomes the principal agreed business of the society, and within that framework of consensus on the great issue men can debate—and vote and compromise—on how next to proceed. Within that emerging consensus and against a background of successful performance it is easier to provide reliable protection for minority interests and to build confidence in and loyalty to the political process itself. As modernization takes hold and moves forward, even over a relatively narrow front, politics can increasingly concern itself not with the question what should we do, but how shall we do it?

Many problems, of course, remain, and may, indeed, be created or heightened by the momentum of take-off. Take-off by definition is a surge of industrialization focused in a relatively few sectors. In the experience of this generation of developing countries, for example, the leading sectors have generally been export industries or import substitution industries producing goods for a relatively small upper middle class market. These latter sectors commend themselves as a point of departure for industrialization because they provide at once a way to save foreign exchange and to take advantage of an existing, available urban market consisting of groups—even though limited in size—which can afford the high prices that a highly protected industry is likely to charge in its early days of learning the job.

Viewing the contemporary developing areas as a whole—many of which have moved into take-off in the past generation—one can observe an enormous gap between the rapidly modernizing major cities and a countryside only partially modernized, if not, indeed, still in traditional stagnation and apathy. This phase of extremely rapid urbanization poses deep social and political problems.

In fact, the post-take-off stage—the drive to technological maturity—in most contemporary developing nations will, I believe, assume the form of spreading the techniques of modern industry, agriculture, and marketing from the cities, out over the face of the whole nation.

In addition to the problem of urban-rural balance, take-off poses other questions: For example, the political process may not reflect sensitively and promptly the increase in numbers and aspirations of the business, technical, professional, and bureaucratic groups which are bound to expand into accelerated modernization. Political attitudes and institutions are generally more difficult to alter than methods of production. And thus the society may face during or after the take-off process the kind of structural political change of which the British Reform Bill of 1832 was the classic progenitor.

It is not surprising that we have seen much political turmoil in modernizing nations. The surprising fact is that there has not been more. And, indeed, there is one important cushioning element in this process; that is, the transcendent loyalty of men to their nation and to their national culture. Despite the revolutionary character of modern technology and its imperatives—despite the need to develop new national policies, new functions for government and in the private sector, new relationships among social groups, and, probably, new constitutional arrangements—there is, in many societies, a residual sense of undergoing a common experience, within the long framework of the nation's life. And, as success in modernization begins to come, there is also a new national pride.

Although nationalist impulses of certain kinds can disrupt modernization, national pride is at once a major foundation for modernization and a potential solvent for its inherent conflicts and difficulties.

VI

Now a word about communism and Communist strategy in developing areas; for the whole story of modernization in this generation is taking place against the background of communism's effort to present and to impose an alternative to modernization by democratic methods.

As a political system, communism can be described quite simply in terms of the three major tasks of government I set out at the beginning of this exposition.

Communism is a system of organization designed to project its power abroad, to the maximum degree compatible with the maintenance of its dictatorial grip on power at home. In order to do this, it must conduct an external policy more aggressive and a welfare policy more constrained than the citizens ruled would accept if democratic techniques of consent operated among the governed. Communism requires, therefore, that the costs of dissent be made high and that all instruments of propaganda and persuasion be focused on the task of generating at least passive acquiescence in the foreign and domestic policies of a self-perpetuating elite government. A Communist government is prepared to settle for apathy or latent hostility among its citizens, plus a reasonable degree of technical efficiency in those tasks judged essential for the maintenance and extension of the system's power.

Communist theory would deny all four basic value judgments which underlie democracy: It would place the power of the state as an object superior to the integrity of the individual; it would accord the purposes of the state a role independent of the fulfillment of the lives and private judgments of the individual; it would deny, therefore, that governments should be operationally subject to the citizen's consent, through a freely expressed competitive process of choice; and it would risk the dangers of the human inability to handle much power with grace by operating through dictatorship.

Behind these judgments is communism's view that it has a legitimate historical duty to impose itself on all societies as a unique system of national and international organization; and, as Lenin indicated (*What Is To Be Done?*, 1902), this historical sanction makes it correct in the eyes of Communists for Communist parties to seek their purposes even against the will of the majority.

From this perspective flows Communist working strategy in contemporary developing areas. Conscious of the complexities and crosscurrents inherent in the transition to modernization, it is Communist policy to heighten them. They aim to produce a failure of the political process, and, amidst attendant confusion, to take over power.

Specifically, Communist policy aims to heighten the typical surge of nationalist feeling that is likely to mark the early stages of modernization. They encourage an exaggerated nationalism in order to achieve one or more of these results which serve Communist interests: the heightening of regional conflicts which Communists can exploit; the diversion of scarce energies, resources, and talents away from the constructive tasks of modernization; and the damaging of relations between developing nations and the more advanced democratic nations which must be an important source of external assistance.

In terms of welfare policy within a developing nation, Communists (while adapting their stance to particular circumstance) generally project the view that no important movement toward economic and social development can occur until after there has been a successful Communist revolution. They seek to divert, thereby, the energies of the people away from concrete tasks of development into disruptive revolutionary activity, while heightening a sense of disappointment with the pace and the unevenness of economic progress, and forestalling the emergence of an effective national consensus.

Finally, in areas where they think the tactic may prove fruitful—as recently in Venezuela—they seek to disrupt the efforts to move forward in the direction of effective political democracy, hoping to profit by the breakdown of public order.

These tactics are rooted in a judgment that unless communism manages to seize power during the complex and difficult transition to modernization, a Communist take over will prove impossible. Communists sense that once non-Communist methods have demonstrated that regular growth, social equity, and stable democratic political practice are attainable and mutually consistent goals, an historic opportunity will have passed them by irreversibly.

The Communists are, then, the scavengers of the modernization process. They prey on every division, weakness, and uncertainty that is likely to beset a society in the process of its transformation to a modern mold.

VII

We turn now to the fundamental questions which underlie this exposition: Is democracy a viable method of government in the transition to modernization? Is democracy a natural outgrowth of the modernization process in the long run?

It is clear that the management of a democratic political system in the transition to modernization is difficult. It is difficult because of the inherent problems of the transition, and it is difficult because, in our time, it is Communist policy to heighten those inherent difficulties. A democratic political system leaves open for free debate and the free play of political forces all the divisive issues of policy and special interest that exist in a modernizing nation; and we must reckon that the freedoms of an open society will be exploited to the maximum by the Communists in order to destroy it.

All of this is evident enough, but there are some things to be said on the other side.

The first is that it was never promised that the successful operation of democracy would be easy or automatic. It is not easy or automatic even in as advanced and practiced societies as Great Britain and the United States. The case for democracy does not rest on the facility with which it can work, but upon its offering to the individual human beings who live within it the possibility and the challenge of expressing their lives to the fullest in a situation of maximum range of choice.

Moreover, democracy has certain important compensating advantages during the process of modernization. Although the modernization of a society requires strong leadership and, even, a measure of planning at the center, it will not succeed unless it engages the energies and the commitment of the citizens themselves.

A friend of mine who has played an important role in the modernizing revolution of his nation in the Middle East, described to me one day how the leaders of that revolution and the people have both had to learn that progress forward was not a matter of magical dispensation by the new leadership—no matter how honest and vigorous they are—but a matter for the people themselves. No matter how humble their role in society, they had new responsibilities to assume: for example, how to read and write; how to apply, each in his own setting, more modern methods, whether it was the maintenance of an internal combustion engine or the application of chemical fertilizers to the land.

Democratic values and the acceptance of democratic objectives, of their nature, encourage men at every level to take a hand in shaping their environment; for individual responsibility is the other side of the medal of individual freedom.

This advantage of democracy—that it diffuses responsibility as well as power—has a special meaning in agriculture which engages the lives of most citizens in the developing areas. If we have learned one lesson about development in the postwar generation, it is that collective agricultural systems, which withdraw from the farmer the incentive and the responsibility for getting the most out of the land, are bound to fail. The slow, grinding drama of agriculture under communism demonstrates day after day, year after year that there are simply not enough police in the world to follow the peasant about to make sure he does the things he must do to make food grow efficiently.

Thus, the responsibility and dignity which a democratic system accords the individual citizen can be an important compensation for the vulnerabilities of an open political process in the transitional period.

But there is a larger condition which must be fulfilled if the democratic process is to work in the transitional period: The major groups in a society must achieve a broad working consensus that the primary business of a modernizing society is modernization itelf; and that modernization must be so designed as to spread its benefits to all the people, while providing strong incentives for private effort and enterprise. When this is clear, debate shifts from the difficult and dangerous abstract question: Where shall we go?—to the constructive, pragmatic, and hopeful ground: What are the proper next steps to get there?

Here one confronts the question put to modernizing societies with great force and fervor by the Communists, out of Marx's reflections on early nineteenth-century Europe: Is modernization not simply a question of the class struggle? Are we not really talking about the ascendency of a small industrial and commercial middle class in replacement of a small landowning class as the dominant force in a society and its political process? As in so many other matters, Marx's analysis was incomplete in its own day and thoroughly out of date in this century. The modernization of a society is not a job for any one group in a society nor are its benefits limited to any one group. It is perfectly evident that to be rapid, successful, and well-balanced it must engage the loyalty of all those who lead the sectors into which a society divides: politicians and civil servants; industrialists and bankers; students and soldiers; teachers and journalists; labor leaders and factory managers; workers and farmers; and, of critical importance, the military and others charged to maintain the community's safety and order, within the framework of the constitution. All have a vital role, and all have a legitimate claim to share in the results of success.

Modernization is essentially a communal venture rather than a class venture, although, as Madison noted in *Federalist Paper No. 10,* the pursuit of communal purposes must take place against a counterpoint of factional competition and compromise centered on various economic and regional interests. It is the ability of a community to achieve consensus on the great issues and compromise on the lesser issues, which lie at the heart of the democratic process; and, fortunately, the modernization process, of its nature, makes possible a distribution of its benefits sufficiently wide to encourage consensus while providing the expansion in total resources necessary to ease the process of compromise. No part of Marx's analysis or his prediction about capitalism has proved more grossly incorrect than the conclusion that industrialization would pass its benefits wholly to those who draw their income from industrial profits. One can debate in all societies whether income distribution is equitable or should be made more equitable; but the most fundamental fact about industrialization since the late eighteenth century is that it has yielded increased real income (and public welfare in the wider sense) along the whole front of a society, not merely to narrow groups within it.

VIII

My proposition comes, then, to this. The practice of stable democratic government in a developing nation is not easy. It is a challenge to the wisdom, sense of community, and sense of responsibility of all its citizens, especially to those who are chosen to lead in each sector of the society. But there is nothing in the historical experience of modernizing nations, nothing in the nature of the working tasks of modernization to justify despair. On the contrary. It is only when a sense of responsibility and participation in the modernization process is widespread—from the cabinet minister to the private business man, from the civil servant in a government office to the farmers in distant villages —that the process moves forward with its full potential and in tolerable balance.

For the fundamental fact about modernization is that it is a great national adventure, an adventure necessary to provide the long-range foundation for national independence in a world of modern science and technology. Before that adventure runs its course—before the potentialities of modern science and technology are brought to bear over the whole front of a nation's life—the social and political contours of the society will be altered as well as its economy. The grand object of the transformation should be the emergence of a modern society loyal still to the best in its preindustrial culture, values, and traditions: a society capable of wielding the tools of modern science and technology in the service of its own ambitions.

This dramatic reshaping of a nation's life is a task for several generations of men and women. They have the right to live their lives during the transitional process in a setting which both respects their dignity and uniqueness and challenges their creativeness and capacity to serve their nation. This is the promise and the discipline of democracy.

Moreover, it can never be said too often that the goals we achieve in history cannot be separated from the means we use to achieve them. The kind of mature industrial societies that ultimately emerge from the modernization process will be determined in part by the methods that are used in the transition. If our common goal is a society of free citizens who are the masters—not the servants—of modern technology, our aim should be to get from here to there by democratic methods.

I do not doubt that democracy is the wave of the future. Every culture has embedded in it—and this includes Russian and Chinese cultures—values and commitments which would set limits to the power of the state over the individual, which would assert the ultimate integrity of the individual while defining his duty to the community, and which would define that government as good which reflects the consent of the governed. I expect these elements in national cultures to assert themselves, with the passage of time, where they are now suppressed; for there is nothing in the performance of totalitarian states—whatever their present stage of development—that responsible free men cannot surpass, and are not surpassing where they have set their minds and hearts to the job.

I do not expect the kinds of democracies that emerge to be identical with that of the United States or those of Western Europe, but I do expect men to create modern societies which conform to their own versions of the democratic norms.

The lives of their citizens will be the richer—and the peace and stability of this small planet will be the more secure—if they can meet the challenge of the transitional process by methods which remain loyal to government by the consent of the governed.

IX Guerrilla Warfare in the Underdeveloped Areas

Each of four major crises faced by the Kennedy administration when it came to responsibility—Cuba, the Congo, Laos, and Vietnam—represented a successful Communist breaching, over the previous two years, of the cold war truce lines which had emerged from the second world war and its aftermath. In different ways each had arisen from the efforts of the international Communist movement to exploit the inherent instabilities of the underdeveloped areas of the non-Communist world; and each had a guerrilla warfare component.

Cuba, of course, differed from the other cases. The Cuban revolution against Batista was a broad-based national insurrection. But that revolution was tragically captured from within by the Communist apparatus.

More than that, Mr. Khrushchev, in his report on the Moscow conference of Communist parties (published in January 1961), had explained at great length that the Communists fully support what he called wars of national liberation and would march in the front rank with the peoples waging such struggles. The military arm of Mr. Khrushchev's January 1961 doctrine is, clearly, guerrilla warfare.

Faced with these four crises, pressing in on President Kennedy from day to day, and faced with the candidly stated position of Mr. Khrushchev, we began to take the problem of guerrilla warfare seriously.

To understand this problem, however, one must begin with the great revolutionary process that is going forward in the southern half of the world; for the guerrilla warfare problem in these regions is a product of that revolutionary process and the Communist effort and intent to exploit it.

What is happening throughout Latin America, Africa, the Middle East, and Asia is this: Old societies are changing their ways in order to create and maintain a national personality on the world scene and to bring to their peoples the benefits modern technology can offer. This process is truly revolutionary. It touches every aspect of the traditional life: economic, social, and political. The introduction of modern technology brings about not merely new methods of production but a new style of family life, new links between the villages and the cities, the beginnings of national politics, and a new relationship to the world outside.

Like all revolutions, the revolution of modernization is disturbing. Individual men are torn between the commitment to the old and familiar way of life and the attractions of a modern way of life. The power of old social groups—notably the landlord who usually dominates the traditional society—is reduced. Power moves toward those who can command the tools of modern technology, including modern weapons. Men and women in the villages and the cities, feeling that the old ways of life are shaken and that new possibilities are open to them, express old resentments and new hopes.

This is the arena of revolutionary change which the Communists are exploiting with great energy. They believe that their techniques of organization—based on small, disciplined cadres of conspirators—are ideally suited to grasp and to hold power in these turbulent settings. They believe that the weak transitional governments one is likely to find during this modernization process are highly vulnerable to subversion and to guerrilla warfare. And whatever Communist doctrines of historical inevitability may be, Communists know that their time to seize power in the underdeveloped areas is limited. They know that as momentum takes hold in an underdeveloped area—and the fundamental social problems inherited from the traditional society are solved—their chances to seize power decline. It is on the weakest nations—facing their most difficult transitional moments—that the Communists concentrate their attention. They are the scavengers of the modernization process. They believe that the techniques of political centralization under dictatorial control—and the projected image of Soviet and Chinese Communist economic progress—will persuade hesitant men, faced by great transitional problems, that the Communist model should be adopted for modernization, even at the cost of surrendering human liberty. They believe that they can exploit effectively the resentments built up in many of these areas against colonial rule and that they can associate themselves effectively with the desire of the emerging nations for independence, for status on the world scene, and for material progress.

This is a formidable program, for the history of this century teaches us that communism is not the long-run wave of the future toward which societies are naturally drawn. On the contrary. But it is one particular form of modern society to which a nation may fall prey during the transitional process. Communism is best understood as a disease of the transition to modernization.

What is our reply to this historical conception and strategy? What is the American purpose and the American strategy? We, too, recognize that a revolutionary process is under way. We are dedicated to the proposition that this revolutionary process of modernization shall be permitted to go forward in independence, with increasing degrees of human freedom. We seek two results: first, that truly independent nations shall emerge on the world scene; and, second, that each nation will be permitted to fashion, out of its own culture and its own ambitions, the kind of modern society it wants. The same religious and philosophical beliefs which decree that we respect the uniqueness of each individual make it natural that we respect the uniqueness of each national society. Moreover, we Americans are confident that, if the independence of this process can be maintained over the coming years and decades, these societies will choose their own version of what we would recognize as a democratic, open society.

These are our commitments of policy and of faith. The United States has no interest in political satellites. Where we have military pacts, we have them because governments feel directly endangered by outside military action, and we are prepared to help protect their independence against such military action. But, to use Mao Tse-tung's famous phrase, we do not seek nations which "lean to one side." We seek nations which shall stand up straight. And we do so for a reason: because we are deeply confident that nations which stand up straight will protect their independence and move in their own ways and in their own time toward human freedom and political democracy.

Thus, our central task in the underdeveloped areas, as we see it, is to protect the independence of the revolutionary process now going forward. This is our mission, and it is our ultimate strength. For this is not—and cannot be—the mission of communism. And in time, through the fog of propaganda and the honest confusions of men caught up in the business of making new nations, this fundamental difference will become increasingly clear in the southern half of the world. The American interest will be served if our children live in an environment of strong, assertive, independent nations, capable, because they are strong, of assuming collective responsibility for the peace. The diffusion of power is the basis for freedom within our own society, and we have no reason to fear it on the world scene. But this outcome would be a defeat for communism—not for Russia as a national state, but for communism. Despite all the Communist talk of aiding movements of national independence, they are driven in the end, by the nature of their system, to violate the independence of nations. Despite all the Communist talk of American imperialism, we are committed, by the nature of our system, to support the cause of national independence. And the truth will out.

The victory we seek will see no ticker tape parades down Broadway—no climactic battles nor great American celebrations of victory. It is a victory which will take many years and decades of hard work and dedication—by many peoples—to bring about. This will not be a victory of the United States over the Soviet Union. It will not be a victory of capitalism over socialism. It will be a victory of men and nations which aim to stand up straight over the forces that wish to entrap and to exploit their revolutionary aspirations of modernization. What this victory involves—in the end—is the assertion by nations of their right to independence and by men and women of their right to freedom as they understand it. And we deeply believe this victory will come—on both sides of the Iron Curtain.

If we Americans do not seek victory in the usual sense, what do we seek? What is the national interest of the United States? Why do we Americans expend our treasure and assume the risks of modern war in this global struggle? For Americans the reward of victory will be, simply, this: It will permit our American society to continue to develop along the old humane lines which go back to our birth as a nation—and which reach deeper into history than that—back to the Mediterranean roots of Western life. We are struggling to maintain an environment on the world scene which will permit our open society to survive and to flourish.

To make this vision come true places a great burden on the United States at this phase of history. The preservation of independence has many dimensions. The United States has the primary responsibility for deterring the use of nuclear weapons in the pursuit of Communist ambitions. The United States has a major responsibility to deter the kind of overt aggression with conventional forces which was launched in June 1950 in Korea. The United States has the primary responsibility for assisting the economies of those hard-pressed states on the periphery of the Communist bloc that are under acute military or quasi-military pressure which they cannot bear from their own resources; for example, South Korea, Vietnam, Taiwan, Pakistan, Iran. The United States has a special responsibility of leadership in bringing not merely its own resources, but the resources of all the free world, to bear in aiding the long-run development of those nations which are serious about modernizing their economy and their social life. And, as President Kennedy made clear, he regarded no program of his administration as more important than the program for long-term economic development, dramatized, for example, by the Alliance for Progress in Latin America. President Johnson has expressed a similar view. Independence cannot be maintained by military measures alone. Modern societies must be built, and we are prepared to help build them.

Finally, the United States has a role to play in learning to deter guerrilla warfare, if possible, and to deal with it, if necessary.

The primary responsibility for dealing with guerrilla warfare in the underdeveloped areas cannot be American. There are many ways in which we can help—and we are searching our minds and our imaginations to learn better how to help; but a guerrilla war must be fought primarily by those on the spot. This is so for a quite particular reason. A guerrilla war is an intimate affair, fought not merely with weapons but fought in the minds of the men who live in the villages and in the hills; fought by the spirit and policy of those who run the local government. An outsider cannot, by himself, win a guerrilla war; he can help create conditions in which it can be won; and he can directly assist those prepared to fight for their independence. We are determined to help destroy this international disease; that is, guerrilla war designed, initiated, supplied, and led from outside an independent nation.

Although as leader of the free world, the United States has special responsibilities which it accepts in this common venture of deterrence, it is important that the whole international community begin to accept its responsibility for dealing with this form of aggression. It is important that the world become clear in mind, for example, that the operation run from Hanoi against Vietnam is as clear a form of aggression as the violation of the thirty-eighth parallel by the North Korean armies in June 1950. In my conversations with representatives of foreign governments, I am sometimes lectured that this or that government within the free world is not popular; they tell me that guerrilla warfare cannot be won unless the peoples are dissatisfied. These are, at best, half truths. The truth is that guerrilla warfare mounted from external bases—with rights of sanctuary—is a terrible burden to carry for any government in a society making its way toward modernization. As you know, it takes somewhere between ten and twenty soldiers to control one guerrilla in an organized operation. Moreover, the guerrilla force has this advantage: Its task is merely to destroy, while the government must build and protect what it is building. A guerrilla war mounted from outside a transitional nation is a crude act of international vandalism. There will be no peace in the world if the international community accepts the outcome of a guerrilla war, mounted from outside a nation, as tantamount to a free election.

The sending of men and arms across international boundaries and the direction of guerrilla war from outside a sovereign nation is aggression. This is a fact which the whole international community must confront and whose consequent responsibility it must accept. Without such international action those against whom aggression is mounted will be driven inevitably to seek out and engage the ultimate source of the aggression they confront.

In facing the problem of guerrilla war, I have one observation to make as an historian. It is now fashionable to read the learned works of Mao Tse-tung and Che Guevara on guerrilla warfare. This is, indeed, proper. One should delve with care and without passion into the minds of one's enemies. But it is historically inaccurate and psychologically dangerous to think that these men created the strategy and tactics of guerrilla war to which we are now responding. Guerrilla warfare is not a form of military and psychological magic created by the Communists. There is no rule or parable in the Communist texts which was not known at an earlier time in history. The operation of Marion's men in relation to the Battle of Cowpens in the American Revolution was, for example, governed by rules which Mao merely echoes; Che Guevara knows nothing of this business that T. E. Lawrence did not know or that was not practiced, for example, in the Peninsular Campaign during the Napoleonic Wars, a century earlier. The orchestration of professional troops, militia, and guerrilla fighters is an old game whose rules can be studied and learned.

My point is that we are up against a form of warfare which is powerful and effective only when we do not put our minds clearly to work on how to deal with it. I believe that, with purposeful efforts, most nations which might now be susceptible to guerrilla warfare could handle their border areas in ways which would make them very unattractive to the initiation of this ugly game. We can learn to prevent the emergence of the famous sea in which Mao Tse-tung taught his men to swim. This requires, of course, not merely a proper military program of deterrence, but programs of village development, communications, and indoctrination. The best way to fight a guerrilla war is to prevent it from happening. And this can be done.

This is, above all, our task in Vietnam. It is an extremely dangerous operation; and it could overwhelm Vietnam if the Vietnamese—aided by the free world—do not deal with it. But it is an unsubtle operation, by the book, based more on murder than on political or psychological appeal. When Communists speak of wars of national liberation and of their support for "progressive forces," I think of the systematic program of assassination now going forward in which the principal victims are the health, agriculture, and education officers in the Vietnamese villages. The Viet Cong are not trying to persuade the peasants of Vietnam that communism is good: They are trying to persuade them that their lives are insecure unless they cooperate with them.

My view is, then, that we confront in guerrilla warfare in the underdeveloped areas a systematic attempt by the Communists to impose a serious disease on those societies attempting the transition to modernization. This attempt is a present danger in Southeast Asia. It could quickly become a major danger in Africa and Latin America. I salute in particular those whose duty it is—along with others—to prevent that disease, if possible, and to eliminate it where it is imposed. They are not merely soldiers in the old sense. Their job is not merely to accept the risks of war and to master its skills. It is to work with others who are committed to help fashion independent, modern societies out of the revolutionary process now going forward—with the doctors, teachers, economic planners, agricultural experts, civil servants, political leaders, and others who are now leading the way in the whole southern half of the globe in fashioning new nations and societies that will stand up straight and assume in time their rightful place of dignity and responsibility in the world community.

X *The Nationalization of Take-off*

In preparing our foreign aid presentation for the Congress in 1963, the Agency for International Development (AID) grouped the various developing nations in a most interesting set of categories, from which the following broad conclusions emerge.

About 5 per cent of the population of the developing nations now live in societies approaching self-sustained growth. In the relatively near future their requirements for abnormal international assistance should come to an end; and they should be in a position to acquire the external capital they need from hard loans, either public or private.

About 50 per cent of the population of the developing nations live in societies which, over-all, have demonstrated a capacity for growth and which are moving forward more or less regularly with their programs in tolerable balance. Whether they demonstrate in the years ahead a capacity to withstand the inevitable structural adjustments that regular growth requires and emerge into self-sustained growth remains to be seen. What can be said is that they are exhibiting, before this full demonstration, most of the characteristics of a nation in successful take-off.

Fifteen per cent of the population of the developing nations live in countries which are experiencing one or another kind of serious vicissitudes, but which, essentially, appear to have most of the assets necessary for take-off or even for some more advanced stage of self-sustained growth; for example, Argentina. What they lack is either the essential political stability and national commitment to the growth process which sustained forward momentum requires, or they are suffering from structural distortions that must be overcome if tolerably balanced growth is to proceed; for example, Brazil.

The balance of the population of the developing nations—about 30 per cent—fall into two categories.

The first consists of societies at a relatively early stage of what I would call the preconditions period. Their essential tasks are to build the infrastructure of modernization in education, transport, power, administration, etc. Some quite considerable period may be required before take-off can begin.

The second category within the residual 30 per cent consists of nations under one form or another of acute external pressure —usually Communist pressure—which threatens their stability and prevents an effective development effort at the present time.

These figures are of interest in several respects; but they dramatize an important fact, central to this particular discussion: Something like 70 per cent of the population of the developing areas are already living in societies which have either demonstrated quite definitely a capacity to grow regularly or, with some political stability and luck ought to be emerging into that category in the years ahead. While many nations are further back down the line, in terms of stages of growth, the fact is that growth itself, in the form of a demonstrated capacity to produce a rate of increase in total output substantially greater than the rate of increase of population, is becoming the normal condition of a good part of the developing world.

In the face of this fact I would suggest that the problem that we confront and shall confront in the developing nations is not merely the problem of developing and sustaining a sufficient rate of investment to produce a regular rise in income per capita; it is the lack of regional and sectoral balance in the growth process.

The simplest way to state the problem I am getting at is that, with very few exceptions, what we see in the developing nations is, as one would expect, that growth has taken hold in certain regions and certain urban sectors, with a marked lag in the development of the rural areas.

It is, of course, nothing new for growth in the first instance to center in certain key sectors or regions. In the United States, for example, the take-off began in New England, rooted in the cotton textile revolution, which can be roughly dated between 1820 and 1840. Something like a national take-off only occurred as we went beyond the Appalachians with the railroads in the pre-Civil War generation. And, indeed, the nation as a whole can only be said to have completed its take-off in this generation, with the gathering of momentum in the South since the mid-1930s.

And the problem of regional stagnation is evidently not confined to our own experience, as the evolution of Italy and even France suggests.

So far as the developing nations are concerned, it is not accidental that rural development should have been generally slighted in the first phase of growth. Typically the modernizing governments are urban coalitions: in the Middle East, Asia, Africa, and Latin America. As urban men, reacting against the traditional rural societies, their first thoughts turned to the more glamorous symbols of industrialization, whether they be modern weapons or steel mills; and, indeed, a serious modernization of rural life does depend on the existence of an initial industrial base and an urban administrative apparatus of some competence.

Moreover, as politicians, it is natural that their minds should turn in the first instance to their constituency, which has been primarily urban; and from this loyalty has tended to come subsidized services of various kinds, beyond the capacity of their economies and their national budgets easily to bear.

Thus, if one attempts to generalize the situation in most of the developing countries, one can see quite remarkable enclaves of industrial and modern urban activity coincident with stagnation or very slow progress in the countryside.

Rural development is proving, however, not merely a social duty to the less advantaged portions of the population, but a fundamental condition for the maintenance of a high rate of development for the society as a whole, including especially its industrial development.

In the early postwar years there was debate about industrial versus agricultural development. Some representatives thought that emphasis on agricultural development was somehow a denial of the crucial role of industrialization—a kind of neocolonialism. The lesson of experience—long urged to their credit by the aid organizations in our government—is that sustained industrialization requires the modernization of the countryside.

There are, in fact, three distinct major roles that agriculture must play in the early stages of the development process. First, obviously, agriculture must supply the food necessary to meet the inevitable rise in population, without yielding either to starvation or to a depletion of foreign exchange to buy food at the expense of purposes essential to industrial growth. This requirement is heightened by the typically disproportionate rise in urban populations, which demand either an increased transfer of food from the countryside or the acquisition of food from abroad. Second, agricultural expansion is required as working capital for nonagricultural development: to generate raw materials for industry or to earn foreign exchange. Finally, a rise in agricultural incomes can provide important direct stimulus to other aspects of development: It can provide expanded markets for chemical fertilizers, agricultural equipment, and manufactured consumers goods; and it can provide a critically important source of increased tax revenues.

The world about us offers a number of illustrations of what happens to societies when these dynamic interactions between industrial and agricultural development are ignored or inadequately respected.

The most remarkable example is, of course, the situation inside Communist China. There a regime committed itself to a program of heavy industrialization, linked explicitly to the modernization of its military establishment. It was prepared to substitute for peasant incentives the massive power of its control system and substitute for an adequate level of agricultural ininvestment—notably investment in chemical fertilizers—only labor-intensive investment, carried out substantially by forced labor. The upshot, carried to a rare extreme by a purposeful and unified group of wrong-headed men was this: First, a breakdown in agricultural supplies, such that the whole vast Chinese nation is living on a substandard diet, and a third of its foreign exchange—about $500 million—must now be allocated to buy food for the coastal cities; second, a breakdown in its capacity to supply industrial materials from agriculture to its industry and in its capacity to earn foreign exchange from its agricultural sector (Chinese Communist exports dropped by about 25 per cent between 1959 and 1962); third, a reduction in total resources available for the industrialization process itself. Industrial output in Communist China radically declined between 1959 and 1962, perhaps by 30 per cent.

The measures taken to correct this gross distortion in the Chinese Communist development process have not succeeded in producing anything like a sustained industrial revival, although disintegration has been halted. Many plants are idle or working under capacity; and millions of men and women have been thrust out of the cities to fend, as best they can, in rural areas where, with private incentitves only partially restored, the Chinese peasantry are struggling to keep their heads above water. There has been no failure in the free world quite so dramatic as that of Communist China, but one can see a pattern of severe structural distortion in a good many countries. In parts of Latin America, for example, industrialization is damped because of a lack of a sufficiently wide popular market. An excessive amount of industry is producing goods for the relatively small urban middle class; consequently industry works with idle capacity, prices and tariffs are excessively high, and profits are not ploughed back into industry. At the same time the potentialities of modern technology and agriculture are not being rapidly diffused, and many rural regions have not moved away from the fatalism and low productivity methods of traditional life.

With a melodramatic gap between rural and urban life, the more enterprising flock from the countryside to the bright lights and cinemas of the cities, where the rate of industrial growth is not sufficient to absorb them fully in regular employment, while they impose on the public authorities heavy claims for social overhead capital (housing, schools, etc.) which inadequate budgets cannot meet—in part, because tax systems are ineffective, in part because income is not rising fast enough.

Further, since the potentialities of modern agriculture are not being applied, some of these countries are unnecessarily sliding into dependence on imported food and are not exploiting the possibilities of agricultural products as a source of commercial crops for industry or for export.

Finally, as an Egyptian friend pointed out to me, the lack of industry working to a mass market limits industrial productivity and prevents the development of manufactured or processed export products—goods that can compete in international markets and relieve the dependence on exports of traditional products with a limited future in world trade. It is no accident that the classic initial manufactured product of a developing area, capable of marketing abroad, has been cotton textiles, where generally a mass domestic market can be developed and industrial efficiency attained.

In the broadest sense, the present state of a good part of the underdeveloped world requires that we take seriously two of the oldest propositions in economics, to be found, for example, in Adam Smith's *Wealth of Nations.* Read afresh, it is a relevant handbook for a developing nation, not merely a free trade tract. One of these propositions is that agricultural output is, in the widest sense, the basic working capital of development of a nation in its early stages of growth. The other proposition is that industrialization depends for its profit and momentum on a progressive widening of the market, with the specialization and efficiency that widening permits.

Although various schemes for creating international common markets among developing nations commend themselves on various grounds—and deserve encouragement and support—I suspect that the most important task in most developing nations is to learn how to widen the domestic market.

In emphasizing the critical importance in the next stage of development of the agricultural sector, I am, of course, saying nothing very new. The role of agriculture in the development process has been emphasized by a good many of those concerned with the development process. Interesting and useful efforts have gone forward in many parts of the developing world, designed to accelerate the pace at which modern science and technology are brought effectively into both the production methods of rural life and into its standards of welfare. The brute fact is, however, that the diffusion of modern methods and attitudes in rural life is going too slowly for the good of the developing nations; and it may be useful for those concerned to attempt to take stock of what we have learned out of our experiments in various parts of the world and to consider explicitly how the diffusion process, now rather laboriously and expensively proceeding, can be accelerated.

It is a fair question to ask, for example, whether the terms of trade—the relative prices of urban and rural goods—are such as to stimulate the kind of agricultural development required to give momentum to the national development process as a whole.

Beyond this exhortation for a critical review of our experience and a search for methods for accelerating rural modernization, I have one suggestion of my own to put into the pot.

It struck me sometime ago that in certain of the developing areas it might be helpful to encourage a purposeful effort to manufacture locally and to market in the rural areas on a more effective basis both cheap agricultural equipment and the kinds of consumers goods likely to constitute, at rural levels of income, an incentive to accept and to apply modern methods of agricultural productivity.

This kind of effort could make a contribution to all four of the structural weaknesses to be found in many developing nations which I have described.

It could put the private industrial sector into the production and marketing of goods on a mass market basis, even in poor countries.

Second, these goods, if cheaply and effectively brought into the rural areas, could provide an important incentive to rural families to increase output as well as a part of the means to do so.

Third, by bringing something of modern life to the countryside and permitting rural areas to share at least some of the fruits of the more modern sectors of a developing society, it might help damp the excessive flow from the countryside to the urban slums. An Indian friend recently suggested that mobile film projection units in rural areas could significantly reduce the incentive of villagers to move to the cities.

And, finally, by developing efficient production on the basis of mass markets of goods of this kind, additional items for export could be generated.

In short, I am proposing that we consider seriously whether the experience pioneered in this country by the mail order houses, pioneered abroad in urban areas by Sears Roebuck and in rural areas by the Singer Sewing Machine Company, might have a real relevance to the structural problems now confronting the underdeveloped areas.

I am, of course, conscious of the care with which any lesson of our own development experience should be applied in other societies with problems of a different kind. It is clear, for example, that there are few developing areas where one could actually use the mail order catalog, given the state of literacy and the postal services. But I have always felt that of all our experiences in development there were three which might prove of quite general significance: the nineteenth century role of the Army Corps of Engineers in what is now popularly called civic action; the role of the federal government in stimulating the development of schools of agriculture, mining, and industrial technology under the Morrill Act, passed a century ago; and the role of the mail order houses which, along with the county agents, constituted a powerful complementary team imparting great vitality to the American farming communities.

I think we ought to experiment with our friends in the developing countries to see if it would work.

What is required essentially, I would say, on the basis of a preliminary examination of the practical problems, is that some foreign enterprise experienced in mass production and marketing, linked closely with local manufacturers and distributors, arrange for appropriate market surveys and new methods of distribution—probably mobile stores, transported in trucks. Arrangements must be made for a maximum volume of local manufacture, and financing must be organized in such a way as to provide something like three to five years for the concept to take hold and profits to be made on a pure commercial basis.

Aside from the general experience of the United States (and the special experience in the Tennessee Valley), Puerto Rico suggests that all this is possible and constructive.

This proposal is, I suspect, more than a gimmick. It is rooted in the most fundamental things we know about the way in which human action changes. Action represents a choice among perceived, realistic alternatives. In many tradition-bound parts of the underdeveloped areas the possibility of acquiring modern consumers goods is not a realistic choice, given the lack of economic methods of distribution where, indeed, methods of distribution exist at all. Nor do peasants in many areas perceive it as a realistic possibility for them to change their methods of production. The objective of this exercise would be to dramatize both the possibilities of new methods and to widen the range of choice that rural families perceive open to them.

Are we, in stimulating increased agricultural output, "cutting our own throats?" Are we, in other words, doing ourselves out of markets for our own farm products when we help the underdeveloped countries step up their production?

In the long run, United States agricultural exports should benefit greatly from economic development abroad. In the developing countries, the income elasticity for food is very high. As per capita incomes rise, these also would be a demand for some commodities which could not be supplied by domestic agriculture. Increased per capita incomes usually are followed by increased demand for protein foods. The United States is in an exceptionally good position to supply the coarse grains and protein feeds needed to support expanded herds and flocks in foreign countries—or to supply directly such protein foods as poultry, pork, and nonfat dry milk. The United States also is in position to supply raw cotton, tobacco, vegetable oils, and many other products. It has been our historical experience—and that of other nations—that economic growth enlarges the volume of commerce.

I would make one additional observation: I can think of no form of foreign private enterprise less likely to raise difficulties in developing nations than an enterprise which, in association with local people and institutions, aims to enlarge the production and distribution of consumer goods for the poor citizens and to provide them efficiently the means for enlarging their agricultural output.

But, evidently, this proposal is not a sufficient answer to the basic structural problem I have tried to define. Moreover, in judging whether it is practical in particular cases, it will be necessary to assess whether the resources exist within the society to generate this kind of production and commerce and to weigh what economists call the opportunity cost of doing so. In addition, of course, we must press on with rural development on a wide basis, accumulating all the lessons that we can acquire from what is now almost a generation's postwar experience in the development business.

My basic point is that the time is past when we can afford to regard industrial and agricultural development as simply competing for scarce capital resources. In many parts of the developing world the initial basis for take-off has been established in industry and in urban areas, but the maintenance of that momentum requires that the diffusion of modern technology, with all that it carries with it, be extended on a national basis and especially to the lagging rural areas which are, at once, a relatively untapped source of food, industrial working capital, foreign exchange earning capacity, industrial markets, and taxes.

Having established in the first postwar decade the foundations for take-off in the developing areas, representing most of the relevant population, we must move on to nationalize the process if we would not risk frustrating the momentum already achieved.

XI How to Make a National Market

If you look back you can see that individual nations of the contemporary world entered the process of industrialization at different points in time.

What I would call the take-off into sustained growth occurred first, of course, in Great Britain, beginning at the close of the eighteenth century with the revolution in cotton textile manufacture, backed by Watt's efficient steam engine. Then, between 1830 and 1850, the United States and Western Europe entered the new industrial game in a serious and sustained way. After a pause, Sweden, Japan, Russia, and Canada were seized with the industrialization process in the period, roughly, between 1870 and 1914.

At the beginning of the first world war, then, the whole northern half of the planet with the exception of parts of Easttern Europe and China—from Great Britain around through Japan to North America—had begun systematically to absorb and apply the fruits of then modern science and technology.

Starting in the late 1930s and proceeding through the second world war and beyond, those who were left out in the first century or so of industrialization are now moving into the same process. And one way to describe the world in which we live—certainly not the only way, but one way—is to say that the whole southern half of the planet, plus China and Eastern Europe, is now moving into industrialization. Its people are bringing to bear on their societies a different range of technology than that which was available to the pre-1914 early-comers of the North; but many of the problems they confront are wholly recognizable from the earlier experience.

Now, of course, these developing nations are at quite different points in the application of modern science and technology to their lives. There are parts of Africa, Asia, and even some places in Latin America which are still quite primitive. Before they can begin a systematic industrialization, they must pass through a period where the primary tasks are education, the building of administrative skills, the laying out of transport, the exploitation of sources of power, and so on. But countries containing perhaps 70 per cent of the population of the developing nations in the southern half of the world have already had a considerable preliminary experience of economic development. They have laid out their transport systems, acquired substantial administrative experience, built educational institutions, and learned many of the most fundamental techniques of industrial manufacture. As you travel from their jet airports to their ultramodern hotels, they present, at first glance, a picture of advanced modernization.

But in this first phase of industrialization they have proceeded in a somewhat unbalanced way, and I should like to describe the typical distortions from which they now suffer. Before doing so, however, I should like to observe that the growth of nations, like the development of our children, is rarely well balanced. It is wholly natural, given the nature of economic development and the historical experience of others, that they should find themselves now facing a series of structural distortions.

What, then, does a typical nation among the more advanced of these developing societies now look like?

First, there is some industrial capacity, usually developed to substitute for the import of certain kinds of consumers' goods. The easiest way to begin industrialization is to set high tariffs or otherwise to prevent the import of automobiles, radios, and other luxury goods which the upper middle class in these countries can afford to buy, and begin to produce them at home. This both saves foreign exchange and permits industrialization to begin, and it is no great trick to market for a rich urban middle class.

In addition, most of them begin to manufacture textiles—often, again, with protection for the home market.

The second characteristic of these countries is that, leaving the textiles aside, the market for these manufactured goods is small; and there is a tendency for industrialization to slow down, once the substitution for imports has mainly taken place. If the initial market for television sets is, say, 100,000 units and a steep tariff is laid down, television output in the protected market can expand rapidly up to 100,000. But then it will only expand at the rate at which those rich enough to buy a television set increase—a much slower rate. Under these circumstances, some industrial plant is usually idle or inefficiently used; and industrial profits are not plowed back into industrial expansion. Profits move off into commerce, real estate, office buildings; and sometimes, despite the tremendous requirement of capital, they leak abroad.

A third characteristic of such countries is that, although some agricultural development is taking place, the gap between rural and urban life is widening. In their first phase they have concentrated on the development of a few major cities which have within them many of the trappings of modern urban life. But neither sufficient capital nor sufficient human and technical talent has been invested in the countryside. As a result of this imbalance, a number of these developing nations have become dependent on the import of food for their cities; they have not developed the possibilities of agriculture for the supply of industrial raw materials or exports; and the agricultural population is not an effective market for industrial products.

Finally, as a result of this imbalance, men and women move

from the countryside to the cities, where often, they remain unemployed and impose a burden on government budgets for housing, education, and so on, even though they live in urban slums.

Looked at in this way, the central problem of development on the world scene is not the gap between rich nations and poor nations: It is the gap between the rich and poor parts of the developing nations themelves. The developing nations are pressing upon the more developed parts of the free world the proposition that they have suffered because industrial prices have tended to rise in recent years while the prices of their raw materials and foodstuffs have tended to fall. This is a real enough phenomena, and there are things we ought to do about it; but their critical problem may lie not in the terms of trade in world commerce but the terms of trade between their own industrial and rural areas. The prices paid in the countryside for manufactured goods in these developing nations are too high; while the prices paid by the cities for the output of rural areas and the total resources allocated from the cities for rural development are too low.

My central proposition is that the operational task of development in many parts of the world over the next decade or so may be to break down these structural distortions, to produce a self-reinforcing agricultural and industrial expansion, and to create truly national markets within these countries.

In concrete terms the problem I am talking about can be visualized from a recent survey made in one such developing nation. It was found that 90 per cent of the durable and non-durable goods sold to consumers were sold to the 39 per cent of the population living in towns of over 10,000 people, whereas the 61 per cent of the population living in rural areas bought only 10 per cent of such goods.

Before turning to prescription for this problem, I might add that we have seen it before in other countries. For example, within the memory of all of us here we have seen this kind of problem in substantial parts of the American South. It is only since the 1930s that the Tennessee Valley Authority area has been brought fully into the national economy of the United States, by exactly the kind of self-reinforcing industrial and agricultural process that I shall try later to describe. In Canada it is only in this generation that Quebec has moved into what I would call the take-off into self-sustained growth; and the same is true for southern Italy and perhaps, even, for large parts of southern France. It is, as I say, quite natural to have distortions within a national development process, with an initial concentration on urban development and urban markets, with the rural areas brought fully into modernization only with the passage of time.

Now, how do you do it? How do you make a national market, starting from the kind of distorted situation that can be observed in the world around us?

I suggest that there are four major jobs that must be done, and they should be done simultaneously as part of a conscious national strategy, shared by the public and private authorities. The four elements are these: a build-up of agricultural productivity; a revolution in the marketing of agricultural products in the cities; a shift of industry to the production of simple agricultural equipment and consumers' goods for the mass market; and a revolution in marketing methods for such cheap manufactured goods, especially in rural areas.

If I am correct, what is involved are two distinct revolutions in marketing and distribution—one urban, the other rural; plus a shift in public and private resources to agriculture; plus a shift in the direction of industrial output. Let me say a word about each.

First, the matter of agricultural productivity. If you look at agriculture in most of these developing nations the first thing that strikes you is how uneven that development has been. In most countries there are a few bright spots, at least. Near the cities one can see the beginnings of modern market gardening or even some dairy farming or modern chicken raising. One can see in a few areas, at least, the relatively efficient production of industrial crops, such as cotton, or export crops, such as tea and rubber. There are, however, vast areas of mainly subsistence agriculture, usually carried on by traditional methods of low productivity. Little surplus is produced from such areas for the cities, and little is bought of the cities' products, except, perhaps, the inevitable soft drinks and coarse but often quite expensive manufactured textiles.

A good deal of assistance to agriculture takes the form of building of roads and communications into the countryside and perhaps the beginnings of basic rural education. Roads and schools are, of course, a necessary condition for the modernization of the countryside, but they are not a sufficient condition. Roads and schools in themselves do not automatically bring about a productivity revolution. What the countryside in developing nations generally needs, in addition, are three things: more technical advice, including advice about markets and marketing; more credit resources, so that they can act on that technical advice; and an increased incentive to shift over to new methods of agricultural production or to new crops.

In the United States our great and continuing agricultural revolution has been based on the county agent, the mail order catalog, and reasonable prices for agricultural output, as well as on cheap agricultural credit.

How, exactly, agriculture in a particular developing country should be transformed requires that one decide in each region what sort of new crops can be efficiently produced and are likely to find markets. Here general prescriptions are to be avoided, although in many parts of Latin America it is clear that there is a potential market in the cities not merely for basic grains but also for higher grade protein foods—dairy products, meat, poultry, etc. Just as agriculture in the American South has moved in this direction in the past generation, I suspect we shall see this trend also in many of the more advanced developing areas.

But this kind of agricultural revolution can only be effective if there is a parallel revolution in marketing, and this brings me to the second required element in the making of a national market.

Recent studies of the food distribution system in some Latin American cities indicate that, with the application of modern marketing methods, food prices could be lowered by at least 10 per cent. To understand the meaning of this in a developing country, it must be recalled that more than half of the income is spent on food by most of the population. In bringing about a revolution in food distribution, we are talking about big and immediate margins of increase in human welfare.

But, even more than that, one cannot begin to organize with conviction modern dairy and chicken farms, for example, unless one is confident that the products can be efficiently handled and distributed in the cities. The higher grade foods have traditionally been sold by inefficient methods to a very small segment of the urban population.

It is, therefore, a requirement of a successful agricultural revolution that not only the producers of food but the distributors begin to think in terms of a mass market with small unit profits, compensated for by a larger turnover and, therefore, a satisfactory return on capital.

If one looks closely at the cities in the developing areas, one can begin to see the foundations on which to build. Experiments in supermarkets, for example, are taking place in a number of countries, as is the development of consumers' cooperatives. But, in most cases, they now supply a very small part of the market. Most marketing involves too many middlemen, with excessive markups, ending up in small shops with low turnover and excessive unit profits. Building on the initiatives which have already been taken and the practical experiences which have been gained, it is necessary that all of us concerned with the development business give much greater attention and resources to the cheap and efficient marketing of the products of agriculture in urban areas.

The third requirement in making a national market is that manufacturers expand their production to embrace not merely the goods which the small, wealthy middle class can buy, but to things which have real potentials for mass marketing. I have in mind simple agricultural equipment, cheap textiles, canvas shoes, flashlights, household equipment, transistor radios, and the classic first-phase durable consumers' goods–bicycles and sewing machines.

Having seen villages in developing nations, I am convinced that, even at present levels of income, there is more cash in those villages than we often think. Those who have taken the trouble to produce and sell in the villages have usually done well. What is required now is a purposeful effort to bring the industrial capacity of the developing nations into the service of a much wider range of the population than has been true in the past. They must begin to look at the, say, 60 per cent of the population now out of the game as a potential market. One cannot develop industrial efficiency if plants are underemployed. And the owner of an underemployed plant is not likely to plow his profits back into industrial expansion. The manufacturer must, therefore, take rural marketing and agricultural development very seriously indeed.

In this connection, I would call attention to a speech made on September 12, 1963, by Señor Raul Salinas Lozano, Secretary of Industry and Commerce in the government of Mexico, speaking to a group of Mexican industrial leaders. He urged them to take new capital to the countryside where they can obtain promising results, because only by means of the just distribution of riches will Mexico be able to resolve its long-standing social, cultural, and economic problems. He pointed out two fields of investment that merit attention and vigor: the production of products for the countryside and the production of consumer goods for the great mass of the underprivileged population. At the same time and in the name of the government, he urged the business community that it fulfill its social duty so that Mexicans in the low income brackets receive the products of industry at the lowest possible price.

But there is no point in producing goods of this kind unless there are also developed new and efficient ways of getting them out to the rural markets. In some areas the technique of the mail order catalog, which was so powerful an instrument in the development of American rural areas, might be applied. But in many countries the rate of literacy is not sufficiently high and the postal service not sufficiently reliable to use this method. In the first instance, what may be required are mobile trucks which would go at regular intervals into the villages with a stock of consumers' goods and agricultural equipment—as did the old-fashioned rural peddler with a pack on his back. Some interesting and promising experiments of this sort have already been undertaken.

What is required is a purposeful organization of this kind of production and marketing with financing which would permit a protracted period in which the rural population begins to react, in terms of its own efforts to increase incomes, in order to acquire an increased volume of these goods. I am told by an American firm which had experience in the early days of the development of the Tennessee Valley area that it took about three years before big profits were earned in this kind of operation. But from the very beginning, the availability of such goods at reasonable prices would yield for the developing nation a higher amount of industrial employment for the expenditure of a given amount of income in the villages.

Let me emphasize again that it has been the experience of the United States, confirmed by the experience in certain areas within the modern developing nations, that the availability of such cheap but attractive consumers' goods has been a major factor leading the farmer to change his methods in such a way as to increase his productivity and his income.

Industrial development requires higher productivity methods and higher incomes in the countryside, but the availability of cheap manufactured goods and farm equipment can be a powerful stimulus to higher agricultural productivity. Efforts to achieve both results should proceed simultaneously.

This, then, is a four-point program for making a national market and thus solving the typical structural distortions of many contemporary developing nations. If successful, this program would expand industrial production, increase industrial efficiency, and make the plow-back of profits into industrial expansion economically attractive. It would increase productivity in agriculture and raise the level of income in the cities by providing cheap, higher grade foodstuffs. By making agricultural life more attractive and bringing to it some of the fruits that modern industrial methods can offer, it would damp down the abnormal flow from the countryside to the urban slums.

This kind of program also offers a way in which the private sector within a developing country can make a massive contribution to the economic development process as a whole. It is one thing for private enterprise to assemble or produce automobiles, television sets, and other durable consumers' goods for a small, rich, isolated middle class. It is quite a different matter for it to put its skills of manufacturing and marketing at the service of the urban and rural populations as a whole. I can think of no better way for private enterprise to demonstrate its legitimacy and to insure its status in a developing society than by playing its part in some such program for breaking down the barriers between the city and the countryside and making a national market.

And it is within such a strategy that private enterprise from abroad could find a major constructive mission in the developing nations. The genius of our own private capitalism in the United States—and this is also true of Canada and increasingly true of Western Europe and Japan—has been that it served all of the people, urban and rural, bringing to them cheaply and efficiently the best fruits of modern science and technology. Working with the private enterprise sectors within developing nations and in collaboration with governments which, in the first instance, must accept this strategy and play an important role within it, I believe that foreign private enterprise could fulfill a constructive mission in the economic development process.

Applied, for example, to the Alliance for Progress, this strategy could give the whole enterprise a new cast, a new dynamism. It would not alter the need for improved methods of tax collection, for land reform in certain areas, for increased investment in education, housing, and health. But it would supply an operational objective in which private enterprise would have scope for real initiative and creativeness, a real basis for collaboration with governments, and a way of demonstrating to all the people its inherent virtues.

What greater reality could the Alliance for Progress have than if it began to yield a sharp drop in food costs to the urban consumer; a shift in rural production to new, higher quality and higher productivity agricultural products; full utilization and rapid expansion in industrial plants; and a flow of cheap farm equipment and cheap industrial products to the villages? Other things matter in economic development: above all, health, education, and housing. But it is in the four elements embraced within this market strategy that an economy pays off or fails to pay off, and it is out of the interaction between industrial momentum and rising agricultural productivity that a nation develops the resources necessary for ample welfare programs.

If this is the right strategy, how does one begin? I would suggest that the place to begin is within the private business sector of the developing nation. Business leaders might counsel together and take stock of the untapped market possibilities—get the necessary market surveys made—examine the possibilities and costs of improved marketing arrangements for agricultural products in the cities, for manufactured products in the countryside. On certain projects they could begin on their own; for others, they might require the understanding of the government or its active collaboration—for example, in building rural roads in a key area, or granting agricultural credit to expand output of newly marketable crops. It is possible that private and public authorities might decide to work together intensively—on an experimental basis—in a particular region. The aid resources available to the Alliance for Progress might be woven in the scheme where such special financing was required.

But there are two basic points about setting this kind of show on the road: The first initiative must come from within the country itself. The local private and public authorities must—out of their own insights and responsibilities—recognize their problem in some such terms as I have described it and decide to do something about it. Second, there must be some minimum concerting of thought and enterprise by leaders in the private business community and between them and the governmental authorities. I am not talking about rigid planning, but of the minimum programing of the effort required to make the four elements in the strategy mutually reinforcing.

Once under way, I am confident that the aid authorities in the United States government and elsewhere would be prepared to see how, in particular circumstances, they might be helpful.

After examining this problem with some care, in many parts of the world over the past two years, I am convinced that the basic raw materials exist for a great surge forward over the next decade in Latin America and elsewhere in the more advanced developing nations: The industrial skills and organization are there; a considerable initial experience in rural development programs has been acquired; the first successful small experiments in supermarkets and cooperatives in the cities and in efficient rural marketing have taken place. The challenge now is to marry these up and get going; and the challenge falls substantially on the private enterprise sector—the business leaders within these countries and the foreign firms that operate there.

For these like ourselves who believe in private enterprise, I can think of no more satisfying task than to help pioneer in these new settings the application of the lessons we have learned in our own nations in creating national markets which have, at the same time, made available the fruits of an industrial society to all our people and provided the foundation for regular economic growth.

Part IV

East-West Problems: The Cold War

XII The Third Round

We have entered upon a third major effort since 1945 to establish whether or not it is possible for the Soviet Union and the West to live together on this planet under conditions of tolerable stability and low tension. The first effort occurred in the immediate aftermath of the second world war; the second, in the years after Stalin's death; and historians may well date the third from the aftermath of the Cuban missile crisis of October 1962.

Sandwiched between these intervals of diplomatic exploration and negotiation were two massive, sustained Soviet offensives: Stalin's, of 1946–1951; and Khrushchev's, of 1958–1962. To understand where we are and what the prospects and conditions for success may be, it is, perhaps, worth recalling briefly this familiar sequence which takes on a certain shapeliness with the passage of time and the benefit of hindsight.

It starts, one might properly assume, with Stalingrad. From the time when victory appeared certain, Moscow prepared actively to exploit the confusion that the war itself and the postwar years would inevitably bring. Communist rule in Russia was born of such confusion; and, as the second world war came to a close, it became increasingly clear that, despite vast destruction within Russia, its rulers looked to the postwar period as an interval of opportunity for expansion, based in part on the disposition of the Red Army and the leverage this provided.

How far expansion could go depended, of course, on how the then overwhelming power of the United States would be deployed. In 1945–1946 Stalin evidently judged that the United States was, in fact, behaving as President Roosevelt told him it would behave when he predicted the United States could not maintain troops abroad for more than two years after the war. We negotiated about Europe and China against a background of hasty, drastic, unilateral demobilization.

Assessing his opportunities hopefully, Stalin made clear in his tough speech of February 9, 1946, that he regarded the days ahead as a period for the extension of Communist power. And he mounted a sustained offensive, first in the West, then in the East. In the West, Stalin, although set back in Iran, increased Soviet pressure against Turkey by diplomacy and threat during the summer of 1946; in Greece, by supporting substantial guerrilla warfare; and in Italy and France, by vigorous Communist party efforts to gain parliamentary power. In 1947 he accelerated the movement toward total control in Eastern Europe, symbolized by the creation of the Cominform in September 1947. He succeeded in Prague (February 1948), but failed in Belgrade, where Tito's defection was announced in June 1948.

But from early 1947 the Western counterattack began with the Truman Doctrine and the Marshall Plan. The election in April 1948 saved Italy, and the Communist effort in Greece fell apart in the face of the Greek effort and Communist schisms. France found a group of center parties capable of governing, if uncertainly, and containing the domestic Communist menace.

Germany drifted, from the spring of 1946, toward a split; and the resulting deadlock in the Berlin Control Council was dramatized by the Soviet walkout on March 20, 1948, which set the stage for the full blockade on the ground three months later. The success of the airlift ended, in effect, Stalin's main thrust to the West. The interacting process set in motion by this offensive, however, had yielded not merely the Marshall Plan but the Brussels Pact (September 1948), NATO (March 1949), and the creation (May 1949) of the Federal Republic of Germany with its close ties to West Berlin.

As this duel in the West proceeded, Stalin launched an offensive in the East which can be roughly dated from the activist injunctions of Zhdanov to the Communist parties in Asia at the founding meeting of the Cominform in September 1947. Open guerilla warfare began in Indochina as early as November 1946; in Burma, in April 1948; in Malaya, in June; and in Indonesia and the Philippines, in the autumn. The Indian and Japanese Communist parties, with less scope for guerrilla action, nevertheless sharply increased their militancy in 1948. As victory was won in China in November 1949 (contrary to Stalin's earlier expectations), Mao's political-military strategy was openly commended by the Cominform to the Communist parties in those areas where guerrilla operations were under way. The meeting of Stalin and Mao early in 1950 undoubtedly confirmed the ambitious Asian strategy and planned its climax in the form of the North Korean invasion of South Korea, which took place at the end of June 1950.

The American and United Nations response to the invasion of South Korea, the landings at Inchon, the march to the Yalu, the Chinese Communist entrance into the war, and the successful United Nations defense against massive Chinese assault in April–May 1951 at the thirty-eighth parallel brought this phase of military and quasi-military Communist effort throughout Asia to a gradual end. Neither Moscow nor Peiping was willing to undertake all-out war or even to accept the cost of a continued Korean offensive. And elsewhere the bright Communist hopes of 1946–47 had dimmed. Nowhere in Asia was Mao's success repeated. Indonesia, Burma, and the Philippines largely overcame their guerrillas. At great cost to Britain, the Malayan guerrillas were contained and driven back. Only in Indochina did local conditions favor real Communist momentum; but Ho Chi Minh was finally forced to settle for half a victory (Geneva, 1954) in the wake of Stalin's death and in the shadow of possible United States intervention.

Where were we, then, when the truce negotiations on Korea

began in the summer of 1951? Stalin had consolidated Eastern Europe; Mao, China. But the global balance of power still lay—even if precariously—with the free world. And the West, led by the United States, had answered three basic questions which underlay the hopes of Communist planners. First, it was demonstrated that the United States commitment to Europe had survived the war, belying Roosevelt's fears and his unfortunate prediction. Second, it was demonstrated that Western Europe had emerged from the second world war with the capacity to find again its economic, social, and political vigor and, with American aid, to fend off the Communist thrusts against the Eastern Mediterranean, Italy, France and, climactically, against Berlin. Third, it was demonstrated in Korea that the United States and the free world as a whole had the will and capacity to deal with an aggressive thrust with conventional forces across the truce lines of the cold war.

II

Between the summer of 1951 and the launching of Sputnik in October 1957 there emerged a relatively quiet interval, interrupted by the Suez and Hungarian crises, which resulted directly less from the tensions of the cold war than from the dynamics of change within the free world and within the Communist bloc. It is likely Soviet planners recognized that the phase of exploitation of immediate postwar opportunities was over; and the positions taken at the Nineteenth Party Congress in October 1952 in Moscow reflected thoughts about a new, longer-run Communist strategy. Then Stalin's death intervened, yielding some four years of quiet struggle for power. It was only in 1957 that Khrushchev established unambiguous control over the machinery of the Soviet government as well as over the Communist party. There were also significant and absorbing changes in policy within the Soviet Union and adjustments within the satellite empire, yielding the Gomulka regime in

Poland in October 1956 and the Hungarian revolution later in that year.

There evidently was also some thought given to the possibilities of accommodation with the West. As noted above, the Indochinese War was brought to a formal close, Moscow acquiesced in the Trieste settlement, and Austria was granted its freedom in neutrality (July 1955). But on the two great issues —arms control and Germany—no substantial progress was made. The summit meeting of 1955 yielded no important result; and the subsequent foreign ministers' discussion of Germany (October 1955) proved fruitless. A surface atmosphere of relative *détente* persisted, nevertheless, down to the summit meeting of May 1960, which was exploded by the U-2 incident. But in fact the sky had darkened at least two years earlier.

In retrospect, the reason for the failure of the *détente* of the 1950s is tolerably clear. Two major new factors had emerged on the world scene and Soviet policy makers evidently came to the conclusion that they could be turned to major advantage.

First, there was the emergence in the 1950s of thermonuclear weapons and the possibility of their delivery over long distances by rockets. For the first time the Soviet Union was put in a position of being able to threaten the destruction of Western Europe and the imposition of massive direct damage on the United States. Contemplating these instruments, Moscow evidently judged it possible, in their shadow, to force the West to make limited diplomatic concessions. The theme of nuclear blackmail first emerged in Soviet policy in 1956, most notably during the Suez crisis.

The second great new factor on the world scene, which evidently inflamed Soviet hopes, was the marked acceleration in the revolutions of nationalism and modernization in Asia, the Middle East, Africa, and Latin America. There is no doubt that Moscow came to believe that it had deeply rooted advantages in seeking to expand Communist power and influence in these regions at the expense of the West by orchestrating flexibly the devices of subversion and guerrilla warfare; trade and aid; appeal to anticolonialism and nationalist sentiments; and by the claim that communism was not merely the fast-closing rival of the United States but the possessor of a method for the more efficient—even if ruthless—modernization of an underdeveloped region. The 1955 arms deal with Egypt and the agreement to build the Aswan Dam represented the first major efforts along these lines.

But it was only after the launching of Sputnik in October 1957 that the second great Communist offensive of the postwar years was fully launched. It was in 1958 that Moscow laid down its ultimatum on Berlin. It was in 1958 that the Communist party in Hanoi announced it would undertake a guerrilla war in South Vietnam. Soon afterward the Pathet Lao, with the active help of Communist North Vietnam, resumed their effort to take over Laos. It was in these first post-Sputnik years that the Soviets sought to exploit the potentialities for acquiring in the Congo a Communist base for operations in central Africa; it was then that they invested a billion dollars in military aid in an effort to induce friction, if not war, between Indonesia and the Netherlands over West New Guinea and also to strengthen Soviet influence and the Communist position in Indonesia. It was also at the end of 1958 that Castro took over in Cuba.

At two points the forward momentum of the post-Sputnik Communist thrust was slowed down by major and successful United States actions: in the Lebanon-Jordan and Quemoy-Matsu crises of 1958. But, as of January 1961, Khrushchev's offensive had considerable momentum in Southeast Asia, Africa, and Latin America.

III

The first charge on the Kennedy administration in 1961—somewhat like the challenge faced by the Truman administration early in 1947—was to turn back this Communist offensive by demonstrating that the two hypotheses on which it was built were not viable. Roughly speaking, between May 1961, when a precarious ceasefire in Laos was arranged, and the October 1962 missile crisis in Cuba, the task was substantially accomplished.

The answer to the first question posed by Soviet policy—our possible vulnerability to nuclear blackmail—was given by the whole course of the Berlin affair in 1961–1962, including especially the President's July 1961 speech and the subsequent military build-up. After the failure of the Soviet effort in February–March 1962 to crack the unity of the Western alliance by intruding into the Berlin air corridors, Moscow apparently judged the Berlin position of the West too difficult to undermine directly. The Cuban missile gambit was then mounted, and its denouement brought to an end, for the time being at least, the notion that vital interests of the free world would be surrendered under the threat of nuclear war.

The answer to the second question—concerning the ability of the West to avoid Communist takeover in the underdeveloped areas—had to be given at many points by many devices: in Laos, by an evident determination to frustrate a Communist takeover; in Vietnam, by the mounting from December 1961 of a massively enlarged counterinsurgency program; in Indonesia, by the successful negotiation over West New Guinea by the Netherlands and Indonesian governments; in Africa, by the whole cast of our approach to the new African nations—in particular, our support for the United Nations effort in the Congo; in Latin America, the isolation of Communist Cuba, combined with the Alliance for Progress.

By the end of the Cuban missile crisis in the autumn of 1962, the momentum had drained out of Khrushchev's post-Sputnik offensive, despite the unresolved crises in Cuba and Southeast Asia.

In the course of this sequence, situations emerged which were bound to affect the future of Soviet policy. First, Western Europe continued to display an astonishing economic momentum, not matched since 1914; and it moved toward great-power status, with a strong likelihood of expansion, in one form or another, of its nuclear role.

Second, quite aside from the efforts of the United States to deal with the major dimensions of the Communist thrust into underdeveloped areas, those nations and peoples demonstrated a capacity to defend their independence with increasing skill and determination and with an increased understanding of Communist objectives and methods. The over-all trend of recent events in Asia, the Middle East, Africa, and Latin America, while still marked by dangerous instability capable of Communist exploitation, made the notion of Moscow control over these areas an increasingly unrealistic prospect.

Third, within the Communist bloc the assertion of nationalist impulses—notably in the Sino-Soviet split, but elsewhere as well—shattered the intellectual unity and organizational discipline of the international Communist movement. The process also yielded the possibility that the Chinese Communists might emerge with some kind of independent nuclear capability within a time span relevant to current planning.

Fourth, quite aside from the chronic inability of Communist nations to grow food efficiently, a marked industrial deceleration began to take hold in the Soviet Union and Eastern Europe as the heavy-industry sectors on which postwar momentum was built ran their inevitable course. In 1962 the countries of NATO had an average growth rate of 4.8 per cent of gross national product; the Communist bloc—leaving wallowing

Communist China aside—3.6 per cent. The effect of this deceleration, which has brought the over-all Soviet growth rate down in recent years from something like 7 per cent to just about 4 per cent, is to reduce the annual increment of Soviet resources available for allocation to military, foreign policy, and domestic purposes, although the declining industrial growth rate is still quite high. (The United States over-all growth rate figure for 1962, as we continued to emerge from recession, was a better than average 5.4 per cent.)

Finally, while Moscow's post-Sputnik offensive was being conducted with great éclat and considerable acceptance of risk, long-run trends operating in Russia and Eastern Europe tended to liberalize somewhat those societies as well as to strengthen nationalist strands within them and the popular will for peace.

This, as nearly as we can understand it, is the setting in which the third major round of postwar negotiations is being undertaken.

IV

There is a sense in which the fundamental diplomatic issues and problems involved remain precisely what they were in the immediate postwar days. The fundamental issues are arms control and Germany. The fundamental problems are the unwillingness of the Soviet Union to accept the kind of inspection and international control required to get a serious grip on the arms race, and the Soviet unwillingness to accept a clear separation of its legitimate national security interests in Central Europe from its ideological commitment to hold East Germany as a Communist state against the will of its people. In 1945–1946 the diplomatic issues were dramatized by the Baruch proposal for international control of atomic energy and by Secretary of State James Byrnes' proposal for a fifty-year German disarmament treaty to be applied to a German nation unified by free elections.

In the 1950s, in a world already complicated by nuclear weapons produced in three countries, the issues were embedded in complex arms control negotiations designed to roll back the history of the arms race. But at their core was still the problem of inspection, dramatized by President Eisenhower's 1955 proposal for mutual aerial surveillance. Similarly, the German question assumed a different form with the emergence of the Federal Republic of Germany fully a part of NATO, and with the emergence of the German Democratic Republic to the East. The required effort to reshape, if not to roll back, history was reflected in the package proposal for disarmament by stages that was presented in Geneva in May 1959. But the root of the matter remained the problem of free political choice by all the people of Germany and an evenhanded European security system.

Neither in 1945–1946 nor during the 1950s was the Soviet Union prepared to seek a higher degree of national security for Russia at the expense of effective international measures of inspection; nor was it prepared to accept a solution which would remove the dangerous tensions from Central Europe at the risk of even slowly staged corrosion of communism in East Germany.

These two great unresolved issues pose for those responsible in Moscow the same question which the Chinese Communists have put to them with such brutal candor: Is the policy of the Soviet Union to be a policy rooted in the interests of the Russian nation and its people? Or is it to be a policy rooted in an abiding effort to spread the cause of communism over the face of the earth? In the end, this remains the relevant question.

As of the present time no one can say with confidence whether the Soviet Union is prepared to move toward a definitive settlement of the critical issues of arms control and disarmament—which evidently require mutual inspection—or toward a system of mutual security combined with the right of self-determination in Central Europe.

The objective case for effectively controlling the arms race and easing the dangers to all represented by the Ulbricht regime is strong, even viewed from Moscow's perspective. The first steps resulting from the limited test ban could lead on, with patience, toward more solid results. But one cannot expect men of the age, history, and commitment of Khrushchev and his colleagues suddenly to undertake the revolutionary transformations which a stable peace demands. We must allow time and the workings of process rather than *coups de théâtre.*

On the other hand, the whole of the story since Stalingrad has in it important lessons for the West.

First, we must reckon that the impulse in Moscow to seek the expansion of Communist power is so deeply rooted and institutionalized that Soviet leaders will feel almost an historical duty to exploit gaps in the capacity, unity, and will of the West. The five basic questions which we had to answer in the course of Stalin's and Khrushchev's offensives we must be prepared to answer again and again. That is, the United States commitment to the security of the Western world must remain firm; Western Europe must continue to demonstrate its economic, social, and political viability; the whole of the West must be prepared to deal effectively with any Communist thrust across the frontiers of the cold war; we must continue the still incomplete demonstration in the underdeveloped areas that, with our help, these peoples and governments can maintain their independence and move on to build and shape modern societies in conformity with their own traditions, cultures, and ambitions; and, above all, the West must continue so to equip itself and so to behave as to make nuclear blackmail a counterproductive diplomatic or military technique.

Second, in a world where, as the result of the burgeoning energies of nations and peoples in many quarters, power and authority are becoming diffused, we, as leaders of the West, must conduct this sequence of explorations in ways which respect not merely the interests of other governments but their proper desire for consultation and a voice in the outcome. Only over a very narrow range of issues, indeed, is this still, in fact, a bipolar world. The agreement of Washington and Moscow is necessary to make a framework for peace, but its substance must take into account the interests and engage the energies of many peoples.

Third, the solutions that we propose must encourage the Soviet Union—and, indeed, other nations with Communist governments—to perceive that the world we in the West are trying to create by our own efforts and by negotiation has a place of dignity for all nations which pursue their national interests with integrity, which respect the hard imperatives of interdependence and the rights of other nations and peoples.

Fourth, since what we are likely to see, at best, is a slow and protracted process, it is also essential, if this third round is to succeed, that there be no premature throwing of hats in the air. We deluded ourselves and tempted the Communist leadership by popular overreaction in the West in 1945–1946 and in the mid-1950s, two intervals of apparent *détente.* Very minor progress yielded a widespread sense that peace had broken out. We of the West ought to be mature enough and casehardened enough now to permit our celebrations to match the actual performance in moving toward peace—whatever that performance may prove to be. We could well afford to attach to the test ban agreement the importance it deserves as a major step forward, since we were sufficiently experienced to know it was but one of a difficult series that must be taken for success.

The stakes for us all are so great that this sequence of negotiation must be approached—by ourselves and by our allies—with all the imagination and sincerity we can summon. It is unrealistic to assume that history is static and that we are doomed to repeat failures of the past. But the hard-won lesson of a generation's hazardous experience is that our powder should be kept dry. An awareness of the truly revolutionary character of the ultimate issues—and an awareness also of the undiminished, even gathering, strength and vitality of the West and its values —should give us the poise to be patient. We should make the most of the third round, but not be afraid, if necessary, to await the fourth.

XIII *The Way to Victory*

What should be our objectives in this period of pause which has been earned substantially by the strength, resoluteness, and unity of the free world?

First, let me put the answer negatively. The greatest danger we face is that we and our allies take the occasion of this pause to let down our strength or dilute our will to grapple with the many dangerous situations we still confront on the world scene. As the men in the Kremlin look about them, their best hope must be that the United States and the West may prove incapable of staying the course; that, out of a false sense, the cold war is coming to an end; that, out of boredom or domestic preoccupations or a desire to get on with purely national objectives on the world scene, we will open up new opportunities for the Communists to advance.

Having tested us hard, since 1946, in many dimensions, Moscow may be reluctant to return to methods which were not successful. But communism is not a self-containing phenomenon. We can be sure that any perceived weakness within the free world will be exploited, if Moscow judges that it commands the capacity to exploit it without excessive cost and risk. We must minimize the number of openings available to the Communists, and we must make sure that the cost and risk of their attempted exploitation remain prohibitatively high.

If this view is correct, certain things follow.

First, there must be no let down in our military capacity to bring force effectively to bear. This is not merely a matter of military budgets, but a question of maintaining overseas our own forces and those of our allies required to make the use of force unattractive to the Communists on the spot—whether it be nuclear weapons or slogging infantrymen.

Second, as Khrushchev made clear on the occasion of the forty-sixth anniversary of the Communist revolution, on November 7, 1963, and as the Communists in Peiping, Hanoi and Havana make clear every day, the struggle to advance communism by subversion and guerrilla warfare has by no means been abandoned. Although our own capacity to deal with this kind of attack from within has increased and the ability and will of the governments and peoples in the developing nations to defend their independence have been widely demonstrated, the Communists have not wholly lost hope in what they call wars of national liberation. This is ultimately the issue at stake in South Vietnam, where a war against South Vietnamese independence is being conducted day by day, directed from North Vietnam, with the backing of both Moscow and Peiping.

It is altogether likely that, frustrated in Europe, we shall see a renewed and heightened effort by the Communists in Asia, the Middle East, Africa, and Latin America over coming months and years, despite some Communist setbacks in recent years.

Third, it follows directly from this fact that we must maintain our own foreign aid program and continue to urge our allies in Western Europe and Japan to expand theirs. I can think of nothing more likely to encourage Communists all over the world than a letdown in the American foreign aid effort. Our foreign aid program is a critically important instrument for helping maintain the independence of the developing nations. In the shortrun, the military aid increases their capacity for defense; in the longer run, the build-up of their economies, accompanied by measures that insure social progress, is an essential foundation for the maintenance of their independence.

The struggle to help the developing nations through the historic transition from traditional or colonial ways of life to the attainment of stable, modern societies is a long, difficult struggle. The Communists perceive in this revolutionary transition openings to intrude, upset, and take over these societies. They have never been more alert or eager to move in than they are right now. They remain the scavengers of the process of modernization—as they have been since Lenin formed the first modern Communist party in Russia, itself then in the midst of modernization.

Foreign aid, in all its various dimensions, is one of the few effective instruments we have to help see these countries through. I have worked on foreign aid problems inside and outside of government for more than a decade. The justification for foreign aid in the United States interest has never been sounder than it is today. The objective case for a reduction in foreign aid has never been weaker.

I can understand why members of the Congress might, in one part of their minds, find foreign aid a burden. It is easier not to vote money for expenditure abroad than to vote it—even though foreign aid money, in the end, is spent almost wholly in the United States. I can understand why they should look about for a way to shift or reduce the burden—even though that burden has been declining in terms of our national income and is only a small proportion of what we spend on national defense. I can understand the political difficulty with a program which has no organized constituency behind it in the United States.

But history will neither understand nor forgive us if, at a critical moment in a great and mortal struggle, we deny ourselves one of the few proven weapons available in the battle for the independence of nations and human freedom.

The impulse in the Congress radically to cut foreign aid is as serious and dangerous to the national interest as was the impulse in 1945 and 1946 to bring our troops home and to dismantle our armed forces. We disarmed unilaterally and convinced Stalin that even a devastated and war-torn Russia could realistically seek to achieve a decisive shift in the global balance of power and, in time, world domination. To reduce foreign aid at this time is a form of unilateral disarmament.

In one sense the matter is even more serious. Thus far in the cold war the main body of Communist and United States military power has not engaged. Our military strength and that of our allies has proved an effective deterrent, excepting the attack in South Korea and various Communist adventures in guerrilla warfare. But the nonmilitary struggle for the independence of the developing nations is an active war, going forward every day. Foreign aid is by no means our only instrument in the struggle, and dollars alone cannot win it. But every dollar available for foreign aid is useful and will be brought to bear. For every dollar withdrawn from foreign aid, this nation will pay a disproportionate price in the form of a reduced ability to deal with a world caught up in revolutionary changes which Communists seek to capture.

In laying out our missile programs we properly ensure that Communist targets are covered and that deterrence will be effective by a safe margin. There are no such safe margins now built into our programs of military or economic aid. A reduction in foreign aid will simply reduce effective United States power and influence on the world scene.

As Secretary Rusk has been emphasizing, this is no time to quit. This is a time patiently and stubbornly to stay the course —and to do so with an underlying confidence that, in aligning ourselves actively with the cause of national independence and human freedom, we are aligned with the forces of history that will prevail. But there is nothing inevitable about history unless it is backed by determined men. And right now there is no substitute in the free world for the resources and commitment to this cause of the American people.

We must persist patiently and stubbornly not merely with

our part in the struggle to maintain the independence of the developing nations, but also in building in the northern half of the world an effective partnership among the more advanced nations—notably in Western Europe, although Japan, Canada, Australia, New Zealand, and other nations have an expanded role to play in this partnership.

Having fully recovered from the war and enjoyed a remarkable decade of development, the nations of Western Europe are reassessing what their role should be on the world scene. They feel—and they feel properly—that they should take a greater hand in the life-and-death issues, both of defense and of construction, on which their fate, as well as our own, depends. What is at stake—as they move from dependence toward a role of increased responsibility—is how Europe should be organized and what their future relations to the United States and to each other shall be.

It is natural that this transition should involve debate and differences of opinion. It is the biggest piece of international architecture ever undertaken at a time of peace. But the underlying fact is that, as these debates go forward—capturing the headlines—the ability and the will of the more advanced nations of the free world to work together is improving in one field after another—in aligning concepts of military strategy, in the coordination of foreign aid, in monetary matters, in trade, and in the field of political consultation. There will certainly be difficulties and differences of view. But if we are patient and capable of staying the course—in this field of policy as elsewhere—there is every reason to believe that what will emerge is an effective expression of a profound underlying common interest: In the end we of the Atlantic Community are the principal guardians of the great heritage of Western civilization; and in a world of modern weapons and communications, in the face of the phenomenon of communism, in the face of the great revolutionary forces sweeping Asia, the Middle East, Africa, and

Latin America, we can ensure a world in which that heritage can survive and prosper only if we work together.

On the basis of statements and policies emerging from Moscow, there is no reason at the moment to believe that we are on the eve of great final settlements of fundamental issues. If we are to move toward a more peaceful world, it will be, as nearly as we can perceive, by an historical process and not by some clear-cut event. We see no signs that peace will suddenly break out and the cold war come to an end.

What, then, are our prospects in such an historical process? What right have we to hope that, if we can stay the course, history will move toward a peaceful resolution of the dangerous issues which have wracked the planet for a generation and are still outstanding?

The first thing to be said is that communism has moved forward when the United States and the West appeared weak or vulnerable; and we have seen relatively stable periods when Communist offensives were frustrated. It was undoubtedly American unilateral demobilization in 1945–1946, as well as the economic, social, and political state of Western Europe, which inflamed Stalin's hopes.

It was the apparent weakness and vulnerability of Asia which inflamed Stalin's and Mao's hopes in the latter part of the 1940s.

It was the believed vulnerability of the West to nuclear blackmail and the apparent vulnerability of the developing nations to Communist intrusion that formed the foundation for Khrushchev's post-Sputnik offensives.

The first lesson of our experience is, therefore, that the prospects for peace are directly related to the strength and unity of the West and the effectiveness of our policies in every quarter of the globe.

But there is something more to be said. The forces at work within the Communist bloc all push in a similar direction. Nationalism is on the rise in Communist China, Eastern Europe, and, indeed, in the Soviet Union itself. One of the oldest claims of communism—namely, that it is a doctrine and movement which transcends the ancient claims of nationalism—has never looked less persuasive. On the contrary, despite debate and difficulty, the non-Communist world is making real progress in finding ways in which dignified and proud national states can concert for larger common purposes: within Europe, in the Atlantic Community; in the expanding relations of Japan, both with the Atlantic Community, within Asia, and in other parts of the world; within Latin America and in our hemispheric relations with Latin America; and within Africa. Dangerous clashes of nationalism exist in many parts of the free world and absorb a high proportion of the energies of diplomacy in the search for pacific settlement. But building on the most fundamental of the commitments of free men—namely, to search and find collective solutions in an environment of diffuse authority—we are making real progress.

Second, the claim of Communists that they have found a more efficient, if more ruthless, method for developing an underdeveloped area can no longer be sustained. And there is an inescapable reason for this failure; namely, that the techniques of Communist control are incompatible with the efficiency of agriculture in an underdeveloped area where three-fourths of the people are normally engaged in rural life. This is what Communist China has massively demonstrated to the world in the past five years. And its demonstration has been reinforced by the failures in North Vietnam and in Castro's Cuba. There are ample problems on our agenda in proving the compatibility of economic progress and human liberty in Asia, the Middle East, Africa, and Latin America. But there is no reason for any of us to believe that communism offers a realistic and effective alternative.

Similarly, in more advanced societies the more we observe of the evolution of the Soviet Union and Eastern Europe, the more clear it is that communism, as a technique for organizing a modern society, has nothing to offer men—either in growth, stability, or social equity—that intelligent, democratic societies cannot do better. We in the more advanced democracies have an ample agenda. But we can approach that agenda in confidence that events and hard facts—not theoretical debate—are demonstrating that communism is a technically inferior as well as an inhumane alternative.

In Eastern Europe there is also a solid basis for hope. After almost a generation's monopoly in propaganda and education, the young are not turning to communism for inspiration or guidance. In the social sciences they look to the lively evolution of thought in the West; in culture, they reach back to their national traditions, which are closely linked to those of the nations in Western Europe.

In Eastern Germany we see an imposed regime of virtual occupation which, every day, appears before the world as an historical anachronism.

None of these historical facts or trends will in itself, bring us movement toward peace unless we of the West stay the course, maintain our strength, struggle for increased unity, and build an increasingly effective community of free nations.

But if we in the West demonstrate a capacity to persist doggedly along the lines of current policy and commitment—lines which have been built up in four postwar administrations and by a generation's effort throughout the West—we have every reason to believe not only that we shall not be buried, but that the principles for which we stand shall triumph.

INDEX

Africa, x, 3, 6, 7, 13, 21, 23, 25, 44, 50, 60, 77, 83, 98, 113, 120, 133, 151, 154, 161, 164, 166
  guerrilla warfare in, 120
  modernization in, 23, 25, 50, 83, 98, 113, 123, 133, 151
  nationalism in, 151
  preponderance of American role in, 60
Agency for International Development (AID), 121
Agriculture:
  failures in Communist nations, 90, 125-126, 166
  importance in developing nations, 86, 90-91, 108, 124
  industrialization versus, 124-131
  need for cheap credit, 137, 143
  subsistence, 137
AID (Agency for International Development), 121
Airlift, 7, 11, 148
Algeria, 21, 97
Alliance for Progress, 13, 15, 16, 26, 85, 117, 142-143, 153
American Revolution, 119
American University, 10
Anticolonialism, 152
Argentina, 121
Aristotle, 46
Arms control, 49, 155-157
Arms Control and Disarmament Agency, 15
Arms race, 7, 15, 23, 28
  see also Nuclear blackmail and Nuclear weapons
Asia, x, 3, 6, 7-8, 10, 13, 21, 23, 25, 44, 50, 60, 77, 83, 98, 113, 120, 123, 133, 149, 151, 154, 161, 164, 166
  activist injunction to Communists in by Cominform, 149
  guerrilla warfare in, 120
  modernization in, 23, 25, 50, 83, 98, 113, 123, 133, 151
  nationalism in, 151
  preponderance of American role in, 60
Aswan Dam, 152
Atlantic Alliance, 15, 57, 61-68, 79
  development of Atlantic military doctrine, 65
  development of collective solutions within, 67-68
  organization of nuclear affairs, 61-67, 79
    joint management of nuclear deterrent, 62, 66
    mixed manned multilateral nuclear force, 65-66
Atlantic Community, 24, 38, 50, 57-68, 72, 76-80, 164, 166
  American policy before World War II, 57-58
  American policy toward after 1946, 58-60
    dangers of policy for U.S., 59
    elements that produced policy, 58-59
  colonial disengagement, 61
  formation of policy of European unity, 58-60
  nationalism within, 67-68
  new trade patterns between United States and, 24
  partnership with U.S., 50, 60-61, 67, 164
  position of Germany in, 72, 76-80
  relations with underdeveloped nations, 61, 67, 79
Atmospheric test ban treaty, 10, 15
Atomic weapons. *See* Nuclear weapons
Australia, 164

Austria, 151
Axis, 71
Azerbaijan, 27, 36

Ballistic missiles, medium-range, 63, 66
Baruch proposal for international control of atomic energy, 155
Batista, Fulgencio, 99, 112
Battle of Cowpens, 119
Belgium, x, 9
Berlin, 8, 20, 27, 34, 36, 40, 67, 74, 75, 77, 78, 79, 152, 153
  see also West Berlin
Berlin airlift, 7, 148
Berlin blockade of 1948–1949, 41-42
Berlin Control Council, 148
Berlin Wall, 41
Bizerte, 21
Bombers, strategic, 11
Brazil, 122
British Commonwealth, 26, 50
Brussels Pact (1948), 148
Bunker, Ellsworth, 9
Burma, guerrilla warfare in, 149
Business expansion, in the U.S., 6
Byrnes, James, 155

Canada, 23, 65, 86, 88, 132, 136, 142, 164
Capitalism, democratic, 52
Castro, Fidel, 8, 22, 38, 99, 152, 166
Center for International Studies, M.I.T., 98
Central Treaty Organization (CENTO), 84
Chemistry, 47
China. *See* Communist China and Taiwan
Churchill, Winston, 57
Ciano, Count Galeazzo, 71
Civil War, American, 97, 123
Cold war, x, xi, 3-4, 7-12, 13, 19, 20-33, 34, 37-42, 43, 62, 74, 75, 77, 112, 147-159, 160-167
  atmospheric test ban, 10, 15
  beginning of the end of, 19
  crises:
    Berlin, 7, 8, 20, 34, 74, 75
    The Congo, 9, 20, 34, 112, 152
    Cuba, 3, 8, 9-10, 12, 13, 19, 34, 37-39, 41, 42, 74, 112, 147, 153, 154
    Hungarian, 150, 151
    Laos, 8, 20, 112
    Lebanon-Jordan, 152
    Quemoy-Matsu, 20, 42, 152
    Suez, 21, 150, 151
    Vietnam, 8, 20, 112
    West New Guinea, 9, 21, 152, 153
  détente of the 1950s, 151, 158
  history of since 1945, 37-42
  hot line agreement, 10
  post-Sputnik offensive by Soviet Union, xi, 3-4, 7-10, 12, 34, 152-154, 155, 165
  shift in balance of since January, 1961, 8-10
  the third round, 147-159
  U.S. strategy in, 20-33
  the way to victory, 160-167
Colonial disengagement, 61
Cominform, 148, 149
Common Market, 15, 71
Commonwealth, British, 26, 50
Communism, in developing areas, 104-106, 113-114
  see also Guerrilla warfare; Insurrection; Subversion
Communist bloc, 11, 23, 31-32, 47, 51, 52, 154-155, 165-166, 167
  dispersion of power within, 23, 31-32
  economic difficulties, 11
  effects of Sino-Soviet dispute, 31, 154
  fragmentation of, 31-32
  growth rate of gross national product, 1962, 154-155
  rise of nationalism within, 11, 31-32, 52, 154, 165-166, 167
Communist China, 11, 30, 31, 67, 77, 89, 90, 114, 125-126, 149, 154, 155, 156, 161, 165, 166
  agricultural failures, 30, 90, 125-126, 166
  dispute with Soviet Union, 31, 154
  economic difficulties, 11, 90
  effort to acquire nuclear weapons, 67, 77, 154
  nationalism in, 165
Congo, The, 8, 9, 20, 21, 34, 40, 112, 152, 153

crises in, 9, 20, 34, 112, 152
prevention of installation of Communist-controlled government in, 40
United Nations force in, 9, 40, 153
Congress, U.S., 15, 65, 96, 121, 162
Consensus of public opinion, necessity for a democracy, 96-98, 99, 102, 106
Constitution, of the U.S., 53
Consumer cooperatives, experiments in developing nations, 138, 144
Cotton, 137
Counterguerrilla forces, 36
Counterinsurgency program, 42, 153
Credit, agricultural, need for in developing nations, 137, 143
Cuba, 3, 8, 9-10, 12, 13, 19, 21, 30, 34, 37-39, 41, 42, 74, 99, 112, 147, 152, 153, 154, 161, 166
agricultural failures, 166
missile crisis of October, 1962, 3, 8, 9-10, 12, 13, 19, 34, 37-39, 41, 42, 74, 112, 147, 153, 154
psychological and political consequences of U.S. policy, 41
relation between democracy and degree of modernization, 99
Czechoslovakia, 148

Dairy products, 137, 138
"Decade of development," 26
Declaration of Independence, 53
Democracy, in developing nations, 92-111, 122
democracy defined, 93-96
direction in which those who believe in democracy seek to move, 94-95
interconnection between modernization and, 99
necessity for consensus of public opinion, 96-98
preconditions, 96-100, 122
in the transition to modernization, 106-110
Détente in cold war in 1950s, 151, 158
Deterrent power, of American nuclear resources, 23-24
Developing nations:
see also Underdeveloped nations
agricultural development, importance of, 108, 124-131
categories of, 121-122
communism in, 104-106, 113-114
conflicts between old and new patterns of life, 101, 113
creating international common market among, 127
democracy in, 92-111, 122
education, 6, 133, 135, 137, 142
gap between urban and rural life, 134-135
high tariffs, 133-134
industrialization versus agricultural development, 124-131
land reform, need for, 142
making a national market, 132-144
modernization, 98, 99, 106-110, 113, 133-135
democracy in transition to, 106-110
indexes of, 98
unbalanced, 133-135
national interest of U.S. in, 116-117
nationalism in, 105-106
need for new marketing systems for rural areas, 128-131, 138-141
consumer cooperative experiments, 138, 144
mail order catalogs, 128-129, 137, 140
mobile trucks, 140
supermarket experiments, 138, 144
nonmilitary struggle for independence of, 163-164
post-take-off stage, 103
preconditions period, 122
private enterprise from abroad, 142-143, 144
problem of rapid urbanization, 103
rural development, 124, 128-131, 138-141
take-off stage, 102-104, 121-131
nationalization of, 121-131
taxation systems, need for, 101, 102, 126, 142
transport systems, 133, 137
welfare policy within, 101, 106, 143

Development Assistance Committee of the OECD, 26, 61
Diem, Ngo Dinh, 41
Dien Bien Phu, French defeat at, 8
Diplomacy, combined with military action in U.S. national security policy, 34-44, 45-54
Disarmament, 28, 49
Djakarta, 8, 21
Dominican Republic, 21

Early warning net, 10, 37
East Germany, 11, 155, 156, 167
Education, 6, 133, 135, 137, 142
Egypt, 152
Eisenhower administration, 64
Eisenhower, Dwight D., 156
Elbe River, 58
Electronics, 47
England. *See* Great Britain and British Commonwealth
EURATOM, 71
European Coal and Steel Community, 71
European unity, 14-15, 58-60, 75-80
  formation of policy of, 58-60
  U.S. commitment to, 75-80

Federal Republic of Germany. *See* Germany
Federalist Paper No. 10, 109
Foreign Affairs, x
Foreign aid, U.S., 13-14, 88-89, 91, 161-165
  effectiveness in underdeveloped nations, 88-89, 91
  reasons for not abandoning, 161-165
France, 57, 62, 70, 72, 97, 123, 136, 148, 150
  Algerian problem, 97
  desire for American security commitment between world wars, 57
  force de frappe, 62
  rivalry with Germany, 72
Franco-German *rapprochement,* 72
Frankfurt Parliament of 1848, 70
Franklin, Benjamin, 67
French Community, 26
French Revolution, 70

Geneva Conference (1954), 8
Geneva Disarmament Conference, 28
German Democratic Republic, 156
  see also East Germany
Germany. *See also* Berlin and West Berlin
  aid to underdeveloped countries, 73, 75
  contributions to economic development, 26
  contribution to Western defense, 74
  creation of Federal Republic of, 148
  economic life, 72-73
  economic recovery, 69
  expanding role in many parts of world, 69
  failure of U.S. to support moderates between world wars, 57
  Frankfurt Parliament of 1848, 70
  geography of, importance, 70-71
  history of modern Germany, 69-71
  loyalty to European integration and Atlantic partnership, 69
  militarism of Prussia, 70
  military affairs, 72
  position in Atlantic Community, 72, 76-80
  rapprochement with France, 72
  revolution of 1848, 70
  rivalry with France, 72
  role in evolution of world politics, 69-80
  stability of policies, 73-75, 80
  trade, 72, 75
  unification problem, 75, 151, 155
Gettysburg, 19
Glenn, Col. John, 11
Goa, 21
Gold supply, 75
Gomulka, Wladyslaw, 150-151
Government versus private enterprise in development of underdeveloped areas, 87
Great Britain, x, 15, 61-62, 70, 76, 85, 107, 132, 149
  entry into Common Market, 15
  relationship to European continent, 76

special nuclear relationship with U.S., 61-62
Great Depression, 57
Greece, 27, 36, 41, 60, 148
Guerrilla warfare, 7, 11, 22, 27, 28, 36, 41, 42, 51, 85, 112-120, 148, 149, 152, 161, 163
in Africa, 120
as aggression, 118-119
in Asia, 120
counterguerrilla forces, 36
in Greece, 148
in Indochina, 149
in Laos, 27
in Latin America, 22, 120
in Malaya, 149
in the Philippines, 149
responsibility for dealing with, 117-118
in South Vietnam, 27, 41, 118, 120, 152
Guevara, Che, 119

Hanoi, 31, 152, 161
Harriman, W. Averell, 10
Herter, Christian, 65
Hitler, Adolf, 43, 71, 74
Ho Chi Minh, 149
Hot line agreement, 10
Hungarian crisis, 150, 151

Ikeda, Hayato, 24
Inchon, 149
India, 30, 87, 89, 99
Indian Communist Party, 149
Indochina, 21, 27, 36, 149
Indochinese War, 151
Indonesia, 9, 21, 149, 152, 153
Industrial deceleration in Soviet Union, 154-155
Industrial Revolution, 21
Industrialization, 110, 124-131
versus agricultural development, 124-131
Inspection, in nuclear arms ban, 155
Insurrection, Communist-inspired, in underdeveloped nations, 11, 12, 22, 42
Inter-Allied Nuclear Force, 65
International Bank for Reconstruction and Development, 26
Iran, 117, 150
Iraq, 21
Iron Curtain, 52, 79, 116
Isolationism, of U.S., 5-6, 71
Italy, 123, 136, 148, 150

Jadotville, The Congo, 9
Japan, 4, 6, 23-24, 26, 29, 32, 50, 60, 87, 88, 132, 142, 161, 164, 166
Americanization of standard of living, 29
contributions to economic development, 26
expanding world relations, 164, 166
foreign aid, 88, 161
private enterprise in, 87, 142
Japanese Communist Party, 149
Jefferson, Thomas, 97
Johnson administration, 17, 18
Johnson, Lyndon B., xi, 6, 11, 12, 14, 15, 17, 18, 117
Joint Committee of Cabinet Ministers (of U.S. and Japan), 24
Joint management, of nuclear deterrent in Atlantic Alliance, 62, 66
Jordan, 152

Kennedy administration, 6, 17, 20, 112, 153
Kennedy, John F., xi, 3-4, 6, 8, 10, 13, 15, 16, 17, 18, 19, 26, 37-38, 39, 40, 65, 76, 112, 117
and Cuban missile crisis, 37-38
Public Papers for 1962, 3
Kennedy, Robert F., 24
Keynes, John Maynard, 46
Korea, 6, 42, 60, 84, 117
see also North Korea and South Korea
Korean War, 6, 7
Khrushchev, Nikita, 7, 8, 9, 20, 22, 34, 42, 67, 112, 147, 150, 154, 157, 161, 165

Land reform, 142
Land tenure, problems of in underdeveloped nations, 86

Laos, 8, 20, 27, 39, 41, 112, 152, 153
crises in, 8, 20, 112
guerrilla warfare in, 27
Latin America, x, 3, 6, 7, 8, 9, 10, 13, 15, 16, 21, 22, 23, 25, 26, 38, 41, 50, 60, 77, 83, 85, 113, 117, 120, 123, 126, 133, 137, 138, 142-143, 151, 152, 153, 154, 161, 165, 166
Alliance for Progress, 13, 15, 16, 26, 85, 117, 142-143, 153
defense of against communism, 85
guerrilla warfare, 22, 120
industrialization in, 126, 133
modernization, 23, 50, 83, 98, 113, 123, 151
Organization of American States (OAS), 9
preponderance of American role in, 60
psychological and political consequences of U.S. Cuba policy in, 41
Lawrence, T. E., 119
League of Nations, 57, 58, 71
Lebanon-Jordan crisis, 152
Lenin, V. I., 52, 105, 162
Lindley, Ernest K., xi

McMahon Act, 61
Madison, James, 109
Mail order catalogs, use of in developing nations, 128-129, 137, 140
Malaya, guerrilla warfare in, 149
Manhattan Project, 61
Mao Tse-tung, 12-13, 115, 119, 149, 150, 165
Marion, Gen. Francis, 119
Marketing, need for new systems in developing nations, for rural areas, 128-131, 138-141
consumer cooperative experiments, 138, 144
mail order catalogs, 128-129, 137, 140
making a national market, 132-144
mobile trucks, 140
supermarket experiments, 138, 144
Marshall Plan, 26, 71, 148
Marx, Karl, 52, 109-110
Massachusetts Institute of Technology, Center for International Studies, 98
Matsu, 20, 42, 152
Medium-range ballistic missiles, 63, 66
Mekong Valley, 39
Merchant, Livingston, 66
Meterology, 47
Mexico, x, 139-140
Middle East, x, 6, 7, 13, 21, 23, 25, 50, 60, 77, 83, 98, 107, 113, 123, 151, 154, 161, 164, 166
modernization of, 23, 25, 50, 83, 98, 113, 123, 133, 151
nationalism in, 151
preponderance of American role in, 60
Military strategy, U.S., 35-44, 153
counterguerrilla forces, 36
counterinsurgency program, 42, 153
during Cuban missile crisis, 37-39
intellectual content of, 49
minimizing likelihood of unintended nuclear conflicts, 37
retaliatory power, 36
Minuteman missiles, 11
Missiles. *See* Nuclear weapons
Mixed manned multilateral nuclear force, 65-66
Mobile trucks, for mass marketing in rural areas, 140
Modernization, 23, 25, 50, 83, 98, 99, 100-104, 106-110, 113-114, 123, 133-135, 151
in Africa, 23, 25, 50, 83, 98, 113, 123, 133, 151
in Asia, 23, 25, 50, 83, 98, 113, 123, 133, 151
communism in, 113-114
democracy in transition to, 106-110
effect on political life, 100-104
indexes of, 98
interconnection with political democracy, 99
in Latin America, 23, 50, 83, 98, 113, 123, 151
in Middle East, 23, 25, 50, 83, 98, 113, 123, 133, 151
unbalanced, 133-135

Monetary affairs, 75, 164
Morrill Act, 52, 129
Moscow conference of Communist parties, 1961, 112
Mussolini, Benito, 71

Nam Tha, 39
Napoleonic Wars, 119
Nassau agreement of December 1962, 65-66
National planning, in underdeveloped nations, 85-88, 91
National security policy, U.S., 34-44
  combining ideas and action, 45-54
  during Cuban missile crisis, 37-39
    combination of military force and diplomacy, 37-39
  interweaving of military and nonmilitary action, 37-44
  prevention of Communist-controlled government in the Congo, 40
  response to nuclear blackmail, 42-43
  in Vietnam, 39, 41, 42
Nationalism, 11, 31-32, 52, 67-68, 105-106, 151, 154, 165-166, 167
  in Atlantic Community, 67-68
  in Communist bloc nations, 11, 31-32, 52, 154, 165-166, 167
  in developing nations, 105-106, 151
  in Soviet Union, 166
NATO, 9, 41, 63, 65, 66, 71, 72, 74, 148, 156
Netherlands, The, 9, 152, 153
New Deal, 5, 45
New Zealand, 164
Nile River, 46
Nineteenth (Communist) Party Congress (1952), 150
"No win" policies, 35
Non-aggression pact between NATO and Warsaw powers, 75
North Atlantic Alliance, 63, 66
North Atlantic Council, 66
North Atlantic Treaty Organization (NATO), 9, 41, 63, 65, 66, 71, 72, 74, 148, 156
North Korea, 30, 149
North Korean armies, 118
North Vietnam, 30, 152, 161, 166
Nuclear blackmail, 12-13, 42-43, 74, 151, 153, 157, 165
Nuclear test ban, 15, 75
Nuclear war, U.S. policies on, 35-44, 47, 51, 77-78
Nuclear weapons, 10-11, 15, 17, 28, 36, 61-67, 72, 77, 79, 117, 154, 155
  Atlantic Alliance and, 61-67, 79
  atmospheric test ban, 10, 15
  banning from outer space, 10-11
  Baruch proposal for international control of atomic energy, 155
  efforts of Communist China to acquire, 67, 77, 154
  medium-range ballistic missiles, 63, 66
  Minuteman missile, 11
  Polaris submarines, 11, 28, 72
  responsibility of U.S. for deterring use of, 117
  retaliatory power of U.S., 36
  strategic bombers, 11
  underground silos, 72
  U.S. partnership with Atlantic Community, 61-67, 79

OAS. *See* Organization of American States
Oceanography, 47
OECD. *See* Organization for Economic Cooperation and Development
Organization of American States (OAS), 9
  Punta del Este conference, 9
Organization for Economic Cooperation and Development (OECD), 24, 26, 61, 88
  Development Assistance Committee, 26, 88

Pakistan, 87, 89, 117
Paris, fall of, 45
Pathet Lao, 39, 152
Peace Corps, 14
Pearl Harbor, 5
Peninsular Campaign, 119
Philippines, guerrilla warfare in, 149
Physics, 47
Planning, 85-91

Planning *(Cont.)*
difference in Communist countries and free world, 90-91
national, in developing nations, 85-88, 91
Poland, 32, 151
Polaris submarine, 11, 28, 72
Policy Planning Council, ix, xi, 9
Post-Sputnik offensive of Soviet Union, xi, 3-4, 7-10, 12, 34, 152-154, 155, 165
Post-take-off stage, in developing nations, 103
Poultry farming, in developing nations, 137, 138
Preconditions, for democracy in developing nations, 96-100
Preconditions period, in developing nations, 122
Private enterprise, in developing nations, 87, 142-143, 144
Prussia, militarism of, 70
Public Papers for 1962, 3
Puerto Rico, 14, 129
Punta del Este conference of OAS, 9

Quemoy-Matsu crisis, 20, 42, 152

Race relations, in the U.S., 6
Red Army, 79, 147
Reform Bill of 1832 (Great Britain), 103
Retaliatory power, of U.S., 36
see also Polaris submarines
Revolution of 1848 (Germany), 70
Roads, in developing nations, 137
Roosevelt, Franklin D., 5, 58, 148, 150
Roosevelt, Theodore, 5
Rubber, 137
Rusk, Dean, ix, x, xi, 32, 35, 163

Salinas Lozano, Raul, 139-140
Santayana, George, 47-48
Science and technology, 25, 47, 83
Schools, 137
Sealift, 11
Sears Roebuck and Company, 128
SEATO (South East Asia Treaty Organization), 84
Self-help, need for in underdeveloped nations, 85, 91
Singer Sewing Machine Company, 129
Sino-Soviet dispute, 31, 154
Smith, Adam, 85, 127
South East Asia Treaty Organization (SEATO), 84
South Korea, 20, 27, 36, 117, 149, 163
South Vietnam, 8, 22, 27, 118, 120, 152, 161
guerrilla warfare in, 27, 41, 118, 120, 152
Soviet Union:
acquisition of thermonuclear weapons, 61
agriculture, weakness in, 90
arms deal with Egypt, 152
attempts to extend influence in underdeveloped nations, 7-8, 151-152, 162
Berlin policy, 12
blockade of Berlin in 1948–1949, 20
dispute with Communist China, 31, 154
expanding nuclear delivery capabilities, 42, 77, 79
industrial deceleration, 154-155
nationalism in, 166
necessity for acceptance of inspection for nuclear test ban, 49, 155
nuclear blackmail as technique of diplomacy, 12-13, 42-43, 74, 151, 153, 157, 165
post-Sputnik offensive, xi, 3-4, 7-10, 12, 34, 152-154, 155, 165
rate of growth in gross national product in 1962, 89
reasons for failure in underdeveloped areas, 30-31
refusal to permit unification of Germany after World War II, 58
Space program, of U.S., 11-12
Sputnik I, 3, 7, 10, 150, 152
Stalin, Joseph V., 7, 21, 76, 79, 147, 148-150, 157, 165
Stalingrad, 147, 157
Strategic bombers, 11
Subsistence agriculture, 137

Subversion, Communist, in underdeveloped areas, 7, 11, 21-22, 36, 85, 113, 152, 161
Suez crisis, 21, 150, 151
Summit meeting of 1955, 151
Summit meeting of May 1960, 151
Supermarkets, experiments in developing nations, 138, 144
Sweden, 132

Taiwan, 117
Take-off stage, in developing nations, 102-104, 121-131
  nationalization of, 121-131
Tariffs, 72, 133-134
Taxation, need for in underdeveloped nations, 101, 102, 126, 142
Taylor, Gen. Maxwell, 8, 30
Tea, 137
Tennessee Valley area, 129, 140
Tennessee Valley Authority, 136
Textiles, 137, 139
Thailand, 39
Thermonuclear weapons. *See* Nuclear weapons
Thirty-eighth parallel, 7, 118, 149
Tito, Marshal, 148
Tocqueville, Alexis Charles Henri Clérel de, 49
Trade, 7, 15, 24, 72, 75, 164
Trade Expansion Act of 1962, 24
Transport systems in developing nations, 133, 137
Trieste, 151
Truman administration, 153
Truman Doctrine, 148

U-2 incident, 151
Ulbricht, Walter, 157
Underdeveloped nations. *See also* Developing nations
  ability of West to avoid Communist takeover in, 153
  agriculture, importance in development, 86, 90-191
  colonial disengagement, 61
  Communist subversion, 7, 11, 21-22, 36, 85, 113, 152, 161
  "decade of development," 26
  foreign-aid to, 13-14, 88-89, 91
  government versus private enterprise in development process, 87
  guerrilla warfare in, 112-120
  land tenure, problems of, 86
  link with more developed nations, 51
  modernization, 83-91
  national planning, 25-27, 85-88, 91
  need for national measures of self-help, 85, 91
  partnership between more developed nations and, 32
  reasons for Communist failure in, 30-31
  relations with Atlantic Community, 61, 67, 79
  residual colonial problems, 26
  run by Communist governments, 89
  self-defense against Communist thrusts, 154, 161
  taxation, need for in, 101, 102, 126, 142
Underground silos, 72
United Nations, 9, 15, 32, 33, 40, 41, 149, 153
United States:
  approach to arms control and disarmament, 28
  Army, 11, 39
  Army Corps of Engineers, 129
  assistance to Yugoslavia and Poland, 32
  business expansion, 6
  commitment to European unity, 75-80
  Congress, 15, 65, 96, 121, 162
  Constitution, 53
  Declaration of Independence, 53
  deterrent power of nuclear resources, 23-24
  development of Atlantic military doctrine, 65
  domestic policies, 6, 17
  European policy before World War II, 57-58
  formation of policy of European unity, 58-60
  Marines, 39

United States *(Cont.)*
military strategy, 27-28, 35-44
counterguerrilla forces, 36
counterinsurgency program, 42, 153
during Cuban missile crisis, 37-39
early warning network, 10, 37
intellectual content of, 49
minimizing likelihood of unintended nuclear conflicts, 37
retaliatory power, 36
mistakes in European policy between world wars, 71
national interest in developing nations, 116-117
national security policy, 34-44, 45-54
combining ideas and action, 45-54
during Cuban missile crisis, 37-39
interweaving of military and nonmilitary action, 37-44
response to nuclear blackmail, 42-43
and nations under Communist rule, 28, 31
new patterns of trade, 24
nuclear monopoly, 79
objectives of Kennedy and Johnson administrations, 17-18
Policy Planning Council, ix, xi, 9
policy toward Atlantic Community after 1946, 58-60
preponderance of role in Asia, Middle East, Africa, and Latin America, 60
race relations, 6
rate of growth in gross national product in 1962, 89, 155
reasons for not abandoning foreign aid, 161-165
responsibility for deterring use of nuclear weapons, 117
space program, 11-12
strain on balance of payments, 73
strategy in cold war, 20-33
and transition to partnership with Atlantic Community, 60-61, 67
unpreparedness for World Wars I and II, 49
wages in, 6
Urbanization, in developing nations, 103

Venezuela, x, 106
Vienna Conference, 8
Vientiane, 8
Viet Cong, 120
Vietnam, 8, 20, 39, 41, 42, 85, 117, 118, 120, 153. *See also* North Vietnam and South Vietnam
guerrilla warfare in, 41, 118, 120, 152
U.S. policy in, 39, 41, 42

Wages, in the U.S., 6
Wars of national liberation, 22
Watt, James, 132
Wealth of Nations, 127
Welfare policy in a developing nation, 101, 106, 143
West Berlin, x, 3, 7, 20, 37, 44, 72, 74, 148, 150
West New Guinea, 9, 21, 152, 153
What Is To Be Done?, 105
Wilson, Woodrow, 5
World War I, 5, 49
World War II, 5-6, 49, 53, 58, 60, 63, 150

Yalu River, 149
Yugoslavia, 32, 148

Zhdanov, Andrei A., 149